Road to Nashville

ABOUT THE AUTHOR

Joe W. Burton, like J. M. Frost, was a man of vision, a bold pioneer who knew and did what the hour demanded. His combination of skills and interests qualified him to interpret Southern Baptist history.

He devoted a lifetime to Southern Baptist work, including service with the three Boards of the Convention. After several years at the Home Mission Board, he came to the Sunday School Board, where he led Southern Baptists in a new era of emphasis on the Christian home. *Home Life*, the magazine of which he was the first and only editor from 1947 until his retirement in 1972, has touched millions of lives with the good news that can make a difference in families. Upon his retirement, Dr. and Mrs. Burton served with the Foreign Mission Board in an English-speaking church in Munich. In addition to his work with three Boards, he served as an elected secretary of the Southern Baptist Convention from 1947-65.

Road to Nashville is his tenth book, finished just prior to his death in May 1976. It is a sequel to and third book in a trilogy on Baptist Roads: *Road to Recovery*, an account of Isaac Taylor Tichenor's leadership of the Home Mission Board during the era of Reconstruction and *Road to Augusta*, the story of the beginnings of the Southern Baptist Convention.

Road to Nashville

Joe W. Burton

Broadman Press
Nashville, Tennessee

© Copyright 1977 • Broadman Press
All rights reserved.

4265-32
ISBN: 0-8054-6532-4

Dewey Decimal Classification: 286.06
Subject headings: SUNDAY SCHOOL BOARD // FROST, JAMES MARION
Library of Congress Catalog Card Number: 77-8009
Printed in the United States of America

Foreword

Historians have already affirmed the considerable impact of the Sunday School Board upon Southern Baptist life. At a time when *Roots* has captured the imagination of the multitudes, here is an examination of the roots of Southern Baptists' education and publication agency. From these beginnings, we can arrive at a clearer perception of where we are now, why we are at this place, and where we might find ourselves dozens of years from now.

Why Nashville? This is probably the question most frequently asked about the location of the Sunday School Board. Signposts on the road along which Joe Burton guides us in this book give a graphic answer to this question, along with dozens of others you and I have had about the Sunday School Board.

This volume is the third and final one in a project envisioned by Joe Burton when he began to plan his retirement following many years of committed service to the Lord through the Sunday School Board. He lived to complete all three manuscripts, but saw only the first book of the trilogy, *Road to Augusta,* in its final form. A man characterized by a strong personality mix of the spiritual and the practical, he died secure in his relationship to his Lord and secure in the knowledge that his self-activated assignment was complete.

Southern Baptists owe a debt of gratitude to the pioneers whose stories come alive in these three volumes. And we owe a similar debt to the man, spare of frame but unsparing in dedication, who has so faithfully and graphically chronicled a major segment of our history.

GRADY C. COTHEN

Contents

The Meaning of Nashville

The term *Nashville* to the Southern Baptist means something entirely other than a city on the banks of the Cumberland River. It signifies a denomination's approach to biblical teaching in the church. It connotes the development of church educational methods, the promotion of organizations for instruction, and projection of a system of Baptist growth. "Nashville" signifies an ecclesiology of Convention support.

The limited aim on these pages is twofold: (1) to brief the beginning of this unique Convention educational project; and (2) to assess the significance of such a denominational development.

Now in this concluding and the preceding volumes of the "Baptist Road Series," significant Southern Baptist Convention development has been traced through their first half-century in the personal contributions of three strategic dominant characters. *Road to Augusta* defined the interpretation of polity of the new Convention under the strong leadership of their second president, R. B. C. Howell. *Road to Recovery* reported the triumphant victory after war and the near-demise in Reconstruction, through the persuasive genius of Isaac Taylor Tichenor. Now on these pages, ROAD TO NASHVILLE focuses upon the implementation of the unique structure of a Convention when at last Baptists in the South began to implement the design which they had discerned but darkly in 1845.

Events in ROAD TO NASHVILLE should impress the reader that publishing is more than Southern Baptist expression of doctrine. More even than effective teaching. Beyond these very important results of good publishing, it will be seen that the formation of the Sunday School Board made possible the fulfillment of the structural principle implicit in their Convention. To that cardinal understanding these pages are herewith committed.

JOE W. BURTON
Nashville, 1976

1

What Do We Here?

The human personality must express itself. Where there is impression there must be expression. Beyond this need to verbalize is the driving impulse of human nature, even the demanding spirit of existence. Human life inherently involves communication. To live is to verbalize.

The old story about the man who came out of the meeting saying that he had enjoyed himself: "I talked six times," is more than just a funny joke. It reflects the reality of human existence. Any meeting in which one person dominates all the way through, with no opportunity for response from peers, is a sterile experience even for the monologist. That is to say, expression is not just good; it is necessary, and is evidence of normal human living.

That which is true of the individual also prevails as a social reality. Often, for instance, one hears it remarked that a given church, or a single congregation, has individual personality. Indeed it does. A church has personality. A church corporately expresses itself. This is inherent in the very nature of human interplay in society. And it is markedly so in the experience of religion. That is, religion as a deep inner reality must come out in some kind of verbalization, not only for the individual, but also for the community of individuals.

This axiom is expressive in every aspect of community living. Every community has personality. And that personality forms itself in many subtle ways as the community's expression of itself. The individuals together are a living organism in interplay one with another.

One of the chief purposes of these pages is to demonstrate the necessity of communication on the part of a religious fellowship. The aim is to show how that necessity found expression in the establishment of a publishing agency of a Christian denomination. One great purpose herein is to mark the inherent urgency on the part of the people called Baptists, the Southern Baptist Convention particularly, to express themselves in their Sunday School Board. Such a form of communication issued from an absolute necessity. It had to be. A religious community had to find the means of communicating their spirit, their nature, their beliefs, their doctrine, their life as a committed body of believers.

This, in summary, is the purpose of this book.

You will recognize at once, then, that these pages are intended only incidentally to be a history of the Sunday School Board. The aim goes deeper than simply a recitation of the manifest facts in a given period of time-development. Yes, history is very important. It has often been well remarked that one does not know a thing until he knows it in relationship—that is, by a clear grasp of history. The old prophet of Israel knew the significance of history when he reminded his people, "Look unto the rock whence ye are hewn, and to the hole of the pit whence ye are digged. Look unto Abraham your father, and unto Sarah that bare you" (Isa. 51:1-2).

To understand our present, we must comprehend the past. To predict the future and to respond in the present, one must have a clear realization of the past. The study of history is one of the most timely pursuits for the right understanding of the present, and to make valid decisions in anticipation of the future.

That literally is true. And yet these pages are not designed as a comprehensive assessment of history, not even a concise history of the Sunday School Board of the Southern Baptist Convention. Rather, the limited historical aspect is to achieve a good comprehension of the formation of the Sunday School Board—the reasons for its establishment, the rationale in its formation, and the necessity for expression through publication which brought it into being.

Such a limited turn upon the Board's history does require some abbreviated look at background. Thus, in these pages, there will be some, perhaps even more than the minimum, appraisal of the events leading up to the beginning in 1891 of the Sunday School Board. Even before that date there were, of course, relevant circumstances such as those related to the first Sunday School Board (1863-73), to the Bible Board (1851-63), and to the earlier Southern Baptist Publication Society (which existed outside the Southern Baptist Convention before the Civil War). Thus, there will be enough of the background to point the way to the high point in the decision at Birmingham in May 1891, to establish the (second) Sunday School Board.

Moreover, there will be the always-necessary portrayal of the human factor. Every institution must have interwoven within it a man who literally lays down his life to establish that which to him becomes more than an organization. To him who gives his life to it the institution becomes a living reality. So in the very next chapter there will be a focus on this man with a vision.

As related by the dedicated person himself, the vision was in every sense spectacular. J. M. Frost never escaped the impress of that vision which came to him on a winter night in January as he lay abed in the parsonage in Richmond, Virginia. He has told the incident himself, very briefly, and yet pointedly and effectively in his book, *The Sunday School Board, Its History and Work*. In these pages there will be some elaboration of that experience and its meaning to a man who up to this point seems not to have been uniquely schooled for the kind of mission to which the vision impelled him.

One of the strangest aspects of his career, as he moved into the leadership to which his vision drew him, is the surprising controversy. It is manifestly surprising that there should have developed controversy over the establishment of the means of communication which beckoned as a necessity to a denomination. Yet, that very controversy had been anticipated by some of the peers who objected to the proposal made by J. M. Frost immediately after he saw the vision.

To give proper introduction to the establishment of the Sunday School Board, these pages then must deal with that intense controversy. It was a controversy internal in nature, from within the very ranks of the people for whom and with whom the publishing board should be established. Maybe even far more threatening from without, it involved at once the agency which was already entrenched in producing some of the literature for the denomination.

Thus, one definite purpose on these immediate pages is to relate in understandable fashion the nature of the opposition to the establishment of a publishing board. Why was there objection? What were the grounds of these sincere reasons against the proposal? What were the fears that motivated this opposition? Why did Southern Baptists fear the coming of the Sunday School Board? What was the basis for the strong and determined effort, both from within and from without, to defeat it? Finding answers to these questions is our concern in these pages.

These questions lead to another important aspect of the limited theme of this volume. That theme has to do with polity. The establishment of the Sunday School Board was a definite projection of the polity upon which Southern Baptists had set their convention in 1845. The polity had to do with the organization of a convention. A "convention" in 1845 was something new under the sun. Up to that point the structure of the Baptist denomination found expression in societies, not in a convention.

A society was a movement to undergird the impulse to Christian witness through one limited avenue—a mission society, a publication society, an education society, a Bible society. Denominational structure was articulated through the society form.

A convention was a new concept. As is true in the projection of any new concept, this new idea did not take hold immediately nor firmly nor continuously. By 1891 the Southern Baptist Convention had existed for forty-six years, but the convention idea had been so new that still it was not fully accepted nor even understood. In its earlier years the Convention had functioned primarily so much in mission that R. B. C. Howell, its second president, had said repeatedly that the Convention was mainly if not exclusively a "mission society." Thirty years after Howell, the Convention had indeed not yet become a "convention" with a multiplicity of major interests assigned to many boards.

When J. M. Frost suggested the formation of a publishing board, that very proposal required Southern Baptists to decide if theirs would be a convention. Or would they stay with their older concept of a society structure? The under-

standing of polity as related to the organization of the
Sunday School Board is indeed a significant purpose of these
pages. The convention idea had not even yet come to a
firm realization in the psychology of Southern Baptists as
they neared the end of their first half century. The formation
of the Sunday School Board made mandatory a commitment,
firmly and permanently, to the convention idea. Else there
would be the return to the society structure. This we hope
can be seen in these pages, how the organization of a publishing board, the third board of the Convention, required
of Southern Baptists their steadfast commitment to the
convention structure.

This, then, is the limited purpose of these pages: Why
must a Christian denomination form a publishing board?
Why was there objection to its establishment? What were
the influences that moved a man with no experience in
publishing to lay down his life to bring about the establishment of such an institution? Fundamental to every page
is the recognition of the importance of publishing in building
a denomination with a convention structure.

Robert A. Baker in *The Story of the Sunday School Board*
draws back from an attempt to give the full account because
of the limitation even of his 254 pages. He says that he
could do it better in ten times that space or in one tenth;
that is, the account should be either told comprehensively
in full or it should be abbreviated. Baker's very withdrawal
implies a needed limitation of approach, such as this account
is intended to be. On these pages we hope simply to point
out the background of need, show how that need became
fixed as an obsession with a man of vision, and conclude
with valid verification of the realization of the dreamer's
purpose. Without doubt the success achieved by J. M. Frost
through the Sunday School Board even in his lifetime was

spectacular. On these pages we want to see the fruition to the point of that establishment.

What do we here? In this chapter? Hopefully, we have seen the limited subject deliberately intended herein. Axiomatically, there can be no good communication except only as based on a clear understanding of the subject. This chapter has been designed to state that topic, to make it clear as to the definite and distinct subject to be pursued through the following pages. Now, again, hopefully having made that exact theme clear in this chapter, we will proceed to the elaboration of the topic as herein defined. The expectation is that the aspects of the broad subject will unfold successively and successfully as we proceed together through these pages.

Now, in the next chapter, we turn to the dramatic experience of a man who was captured and became possessed by a vision.

"The Lord gave the word: great was the company of those that published it" (Ps. 68:11).

2

"Fire Burning in My Soul"

The leadership of J. M. Frost in establishing the Sunday School Board is a strange phenomenon. There was really no easy explanation of his coming to this role. It was truly an instance of a man possessed. His background, experience, and training provided no singular qualification. By nature he seemed to be unsuited to leadership in a publishing operation. By experience he was well entrenched in the pastoral ministry, to which he frankly was ambitious to devote his life. Nothing in his background or experience seemed to have trained him for management of a great business enterprise. Quiet by nature, he had none of the native qualities to launch him into intense controversy, and yet controversy contrary to his own genteel spirit was thrust upon him both from within the denomination and by well-nigh overwhelming forces from without.

He was the kind of man one would least expect in the role of founder of a publication giant and the leader of an educational colossus, and at the same time a protagonist in a serious denominational controversy.

A student of his remarkable career is simply forced to the conclusion that J. M. Frost from the outset acted as a man impelled by forces beyond himself. He was possessed even to the point of obsession. He came to the task, not of his own inherent volition, but by reason of outside spiritual forces beyond his own initiation, and quite definitely without the propulsion of political striving. The explanation of his amazing career must be found in circumstances that were beyond human logic.

Frost came to his leadership role as an intruder in the publication issue which at that time rocked the denomination. The issue, says Frost himself, had indeed been the major point of indecision for at least half a decade, beginning in 1885 at the Convention's anniversary sessions in Augusta, repeated the next year in Montgomery, again in 1887 in Louisville, once more at Richmond in 1888, and then in the most intense manner at Memphis in 1889. The discussions had been stirring, with many arguments advanced to Convention delegates in these successive years. The question of Sunday School publications was raised in 1885 by the Home Mission Board, which then had the responsibility for the *Kind Words Series*. That Board had proposed the enlargement of the series to include additional literature beyond the one Sunday School piece known as *Kind Words*. This proposal was coincident with the renewal of a printing contract, and the Convention then had established the policy of offering additional Sunday School publications under the administration of the Home Mission Board.

As Frost points out in *The Sunday School Board, Its History and Work*, there had been intense discussion in the recurring annual Convention sessions, 1885-1889. The point at issue was whether to enlarge the *Kind Words Series* to embrace several publications, whether to commit the Convention to a five-year printing contract for the *Series*, and if indeed such a *Series* could be maintained without financial liability to the Convention. In 1886 the vote to approve the five-year contract for the *Series* was unanimous.

Although these recurring discussions in the annual sessions had been intense, even to the point of controversy, Frost himself had not in any instance taken the floor or established a personal stance on the subject of Southern Baptist production of their own Sunday School literature. At the opening salvo in 1885 at Augusta, Frost, like most Southern Baptists, was friendly toward the American Baptist Publication Society which was then providing much, if not most, of the literature for Southern Baptist churches. That friendliness he maintained through the end of the decade, the Society having published a tract and agreed to the publication of a book written by J. M. Frost. This personal alignment of Frost with the Publication Society was typical of the personal relationship of many Southern Baptists to the Publication Society located in Philadelphia.

The 1885 proposal of the Home Mission Board to extend the *Kind Words Series* and to do so through a five-year printing contract which provided an annual royalty of $1,000 to the Home Mission Board, was not then regarded in any sense as a challenge to the widespread volume of Society business with Southern Baptist churches.

In all of those successive discussions, in the five years beginning in 1885, Frost himself was simply a silent listener. He did not participate at all on the floor of the convention, even though often an interested messenger. He was not a part of the controversy. He was not involved in it, one way or the other. He took no position.

Actually, when by an uncanny beyond-himself experience—was it a dream? or was it indeed a vision?—he became involved in the movement toward establishing a Sunday School Board, he confessed that he did not at that time even know that there had been an earlier Sunday School Board (1863-73). Moreover, in his own brief account of the

establishment of the Sunday School Board, never once does
Frost refer to the earliest history of Southern Baptists in
publishing in their extra-Convention Southern Baptist Publication Society (1846-63).

Frost's ignorance in 1890 of the first Sunday School Board
and of the earlier Southern Baptist Publication Society
illustrates the accidental nature of his own entry into the
publication picture. It was an entry out of a background
of nonparticipation and even of no more than casual interest
in the controversy which he said was the chief topic in
Southern Baptist life at that time. His projection of himself
into that issue was therefore startling and unexpected. Who
would think of J. M. Frost as prepared for the leadership
role? The student of history would immediately think of
a dozen other men, any one of whom by nature, by expressed
interest, and by personal training, would more logically
enter into the publishing field. Nor was Frost inherently
an entrepreneur in any arena of manufacturing or of colossal
industry. He was a man of quiet reserve. He insisted that
he was committed to the pastorate and expected to spend
his life in such a ministry. His reserved nature would suggest
to any student of his life that Frost did not have the thrust
toward publishing, manufacturing, or popular communicating media.

Frost's strange coming to this publishing role seems not
as having been prepared for it by nature, nor by special
training, nor yet by personal ambition. Still further evidence
is the fact that he recoiled from it. At the Birmingham
Convention in 1891, after the Convention had voted to
establish the Board, J. B. Gambrell and Joshua Levering
presented a paper proposing J. M. Frost to be the corresponding secretary of the new Board. Frost begged the two
to withdraw their proposal. Out of deference they did so,

the Convention acceding to this request. Not until the Board met later in Nashville was the action taken electing Lansing Burrows as secretary, which Burrows immediately declined. Then the Board turned to Frost, and he agreed to come to the position. He said it was on a trial basis for a few months. Though he did later come to the role, he did so reluctantly, in confirmation of our present analysis that neither by nature nor by training nor even by personal ambition was he peculiarly schooled for that leadership.

When he did come on July 1, 1891, to assume his new responsibility, it was undoubtedly the loneliest experience he had ever known. Fortunately, for the new secretary on that July day in 1891, office space without charge was made available by *The Baptist and Reflector*, state paper of Tennessee Baptists. This space was occupied for six months and then, again without charge, for a short time, offices were made available by the Presbyterian Publishing House, and again by the Methodist Publishing House.

These months of being a guest of other publishing offices illustrate the precarious financial limitation on the corresponding secretary of the newly established publishing board. No funds had been made available to him to undertake this new enterprise. Nothing. No money to pay clerical help. None for salaries. None to pay manufacturing costs, not even money to pay postage.

Frost's own scant explanation of the available resources is one brief sentence: "Money which the Secretary chanced to have in hand, but which belonged to another, was used temporarily to meet immediate and pressing necessities."

The amazing record is that this publishing enterprise did get going on its thin shoestring. Orders did come through the mails. Packages of new literature were shipped. And, at the end of the Convention year the next May, the new

Board could report that all expenses had been met. There was no debt. This beginning is without doubt the most spectacular of all the successes, immediate and later, achieved by J. M. Frost in his administration.

One must simply admit that to start a publishing enterprise without capital, without funds, with no money to pay printers, clerks, wrapping material, and postage was foolhardy. It was simply without logic or any kind of reason to start such an enterprise with no provision of resources to get it going. A man coming to a position like that under such circumstances had to do so under the impulse of something beyond himself that he would never be able to explain.

Further, the sheer daring in undertaking such a venture is seen in the size of the opposition confronting the movement. The Sunday School Board was not brought into existence to defeat or replace the American Baptist Publication Society, which then was deeply entrenched in the life, the affections, and the patronage of Southern Baptists. Yet, it must be admitted that the very establishment of a publishing board was immediately a challenge to the Society. For more than a generation that Society had been within the life of Southern Baptists to such a degree that now, by 1890, and the following decade, it was a very part of the ongoing existence of Southern Baptist churches. They depended on the Society for Sunday School material. Southern Baptists were willing patrons of the Society. To establish their own publishing board would bring about a collision between the new Board and the Society. The two would engage in conflicting work. Who would have the audacity to head an infant new board in the face of the opposition of a towering giant like the American Baptist Publication Society? No one would do so unless impelled from some power beyond himself.

Surely for a man to take that role, or to suggest the establishment of such a board, would do so only on the basis of a compulsion beyond himself.

There was, admittedly, such a compulsion. There was also a background, uncanny, Spirit-directed which brought Frost to the position. He himself related the experience in the book to which reference has already been made.

On a January night in 1890, he came to the strange conviction that Southern Baptists must establish a board of publications. Call it a vision? Call it a dream? Whatever it was, it came to him in the small hours after midnight. "I was awakened from sleep," he writes, "with the thought of a new Board in full possession, and stirring my soul in such a way as I make no effort here to describe, and for which I make no unusual claim." From his sleepless bed he rose before day to write out the proposal. Even before the morning light he had determined to offer his newly written resolutions at the upcoming Convention in May in Fort Worth. That very morning on his way to his pastoral study, he stopped to see his friend T. P. Bell, who endorsed the idea with the assertion that it would be "a clarion call to the Baptists of the South." Then Frost offered his proposed resolutions for publication in the *Religious Herald* of Virginia, a paper published on February 27, 1890.

In his account of the vision and of the paper which he wrote, Frost recalls an incident in Selma, Alabama. Frost and Isaac Taylor Tichenor, head of the Home Mission Board, are the two principal characters in that incident, but a third, significant also, is Captain Hugh Haralson. The incident involved a conversation by Tichenor and Frost, after the midnight hour, at the gate of Tichenor's friend Haralson.

One needs to see these two standing at that gate, and know who they are, as well as the host of the older of the two

Wm. O. Crews, Jr.

two. The conversation may have taken place in 1889. Frost does not identify the date, but simply says that "We had attended a State Mission Board meeting at Selma, Alabama, where I was then pastor." It is strangely significant that Tichenor talked with Frost that midnight, and that he did so on the very subject of Southern Baptist publications. In 1889, Tichenor was secretary of the Home Mission Board, and had been since 1882. Since 1873, with the demise of the first Sunday School Board, Sunday School publications had been assigned to the Home Board as an ongoing responsibility.

The first Sunday School Board had become a casualty of Reconstruction in 1873, its debts and potentials assigned to the Home Board. By 1889, by a contractual arrangement with the printer, the *Kind Words Series* was bringing to that Board an annual royalty of $1,000. By that date the Home Mission statesman was now at the advanced age of sixty-four years. His young auditor was only forty. The older man without doubt was superbly a persuader of men. No audience, either congregation or individual, ever felt the sweep of a more persuasive intellect than that of Isaac Taylor Tichenor.

And at this midnight hour his eloquence was at fervor pitch.

Frost says in his book that he "talked for two hours." Rather, says Frost in recollection, "He talked and I listened. I was sympathetic, but unable to follow his sweep of thought in outlining the future, showing what the Baptists of the South might accomplish, and the imperative need that a people make their own literature."

Writing of that incident twenty-five years later, Frost reports it as most certainly a factor which influenced him to assume the initiative in the formation of a publishing board.

Why, at that midnight hour, did the older Tichenor seek the ear of the young Selma pastor? Uncanny? Beyond human interpretation! It became an influence lingering in the experience of J. M. Frost. It was in the background of the realization that came to him as he tossed on the parsonage bed in Richmond, Virginia, over a year later.

There is significance, too, in Tichenor's host on that night. There was no more prominent Baptist family in all of Alabama than the Haralsons of Selma. Most prominent of them all was Judge Jonathan Haralson, who, in 1889 at Memphis, was the first layman to be elected president of the Southern Baptist Convention.

Tichenor had been president of Alabama Polytechnic Institute when it was formed in 1872. He remained at Auburn for ten years before becoming corresponding secretary of the Home Mission Board. As a longtime resident of Alabama, Tichenor knew the prominent men of the state and cultivated them. He deliberately brought himself into the life sweep of men like the Haralsons of Selma. While Tichenor was president at Auburn, Jonathan Haralson had become a member of the board of trustees of the Institute. It is no wonder that Tichenor was a guest in the home of Captain Hugh Haralson of that distinguished family. In that setting, as a guest of a most prominent Baptist layman of the state, it is not surprising that Tichenor was moved to dwell on Southern Baptist publication potentials. He had the chief responsibility as head of the board which at that time issued the *Kind Words Series*. The one surprising aspect is that he sought the ear of the young pastor in Selma to portray to him indelibly "what the Baptists of the South might accomplish, and the imperative need that a people make their own literature."

Two years after that conversation the subtle and perhaps even subconscious influence of it came to influence a dream or a vision in the parsonage at Richmond. Impelled by that beyond-himself dramatic occasion, J. M. Frost could not remain prone. He rose from his bed to record the conviction even before daylight came across the horizon. He reported that he signed the paper for publication of his resolutions on his forty-first birthday, February 10, 1890.

What he wrote that day he offered as resolutions in the Fort Worth Convention in May 1890, on the very first afternoon of those annual sessions. He had become possessed by an idea. He had been stirred by a vision. He went forward under that impulse to lead a movement not because of identifiable logic or because of human reason, or personal ambition and preparation, but simply because it had been laid on him from without. He had to give himself to it. He did so as a man with a definite purpose.

Recalling the experiences of those years when he was moved to lead the Convention to establish the Sunday School Board and then to come as its first corresponding secretary, J. M. Frost writes in relating his own connection with that movement: "My experiences of those days were as intense as fire burning in my soul" (*The Sunday School Board, Its History and Work. p. 14*).

On a bronze tablet which hangs outside the Founder's Room at the Sunday School Board in Nashville is this summation of J. M. Frost's part in founding the Board:

Divinely led,
His faith conceived it,
His genius planned it,
His courage built it.

3

What the Man Did Not Know

The surprising disclosure that at the beginning of his effort which led to the establishment of the Sunday School Board, he did not know of the existence of an earlier Board by the same title is confessed by J. M. Frost himself. That admission is fairly startling when one contemplates the fact that it applies to the beginning of a publishing enterprise. The admission reveals an obvious weakness and also a strength.

The language of the disclosure is clear and pointed: "At the time of writing my first article, I did not know there had been the former Sunday School Board" (*The Sunday School Board, Its History and Work,* p.16).

This self-confessed ignorance manifestly was an obvious weakness. One is obliged to assume that the proponent of a publishing venture would do so fully fortified with thorough research of previous publishing efforts. Such knowledge, through careful research, one must surmise as basic in any responsible proposal for an educational institution in publishing. This assumption at the present is more strongly implied in the record of competent leadership which has followed in these latter years. Even at the outset, it would be the obvious assumption to expect an advocate of an educational publishing venture to bring forth this proposal out of personal study of what had gone before.

Now, following the many years of dependable educational effort in publishing, known by the reader today, it would be even more normally assumed that the Board's beginning was based on complete knowledge of what had gone before.

Frost's very ignorance of the past gave strength to the proposal—strength at the moment that the proposal was offered, and strength also in the tenacity of effort in the fulfillment of the proposal. At the moment it betokened an absence of emotional bias which at that time would have done much to defeat the proposal. Frost himself reports in the book referred to above that he was well aware of the current biases. His own proposal brought to the issue a welcome freedom from these biases. He did not know of the earlier Board. That would imply that he was also ignorant of still earlier historical background. This very freshness of approach was at the moment a glad relief from the complexity of emotions which characterized the usual approaches to the issue. Frost came with an innocence that disarmed those who had been locked in emotional debate. His proposal did not carry previous experience or even scientific study from mature research.

In reality, this ignorance of the past is the strongest evidence of the primary qualification that Frost brought to the movement. He came not from thorough research fortified by knowledge, but rather with a conviction, even based on a vision, a stirring impression which awakened him in the midst of the night, and enveloped him so fully that he rose from his sleepless bed to write the resolutions which he was determined to offer at the forthcoming 1890 Convention in Fort Worth. It was the strongest evidence that he was moved, not by human considerations, but by an impulse from beyond himself. This, as clearly proved by later developments, was his strongest qualification to be the leader of the new publishing enterprise.

Thus, Frost's ignorance was both strength and also weakness to his effort. This will most surely be apparent from some summary knowledge of what had gone before.

The first Sunday School Board had been established in 1863, in the tragic years of the Civil War. It had come into being primarily under the strong influence of two professors at the Southern Baptist Seminary in Greenville, South Carolina, Basil Manly, Jr. and John A. Broadus. The first became president; the second, corresponding secretary of the Sunday School Board which the Convention created in 1863. It was under their strong influence that the historical paper *Kind Words* came into existence. It is altogether possible that the title of this Sunday School paper was introduced to suggest the need for every influence that might bring peace to a warring nation. It was published continuously almost to the present century. Its title, as a phrase, has been well known in publishing annals of Southern Baptist even to the present.

Unfortunately, however, the desire for peace even among Southern Baptists was not to be realized through *Kind Words*. Midway of its brief ten-year span of existence, the first Sunday School Board was removed to Memphis, and there became embroiled in the upsetting Landmark controversy raging at the time. Ultimately, that Sunday School Board in Memphis came under the leadership of a longtime Landmarker, a man by the name of T. C. Teasdale. Moreover, the Board piled up debts that were frightening—the then staggering total of some $8,000.

In consequence of these interrelated factors, that first Board ultimately was abolished, its liabilities and responsibilities being assigned to the Home Mission Board, which was still called the Board of Domestic Missions and was located in Marion, Alabama. Yet, it must be quickly admitted that the potential assets of the publication venture did become financially profitable even to the Home Mission Board. By frugal management, as well as from realization of financial potential in the distribution of Sunday School literature, the big debt was fully paid and the publications (which were ultimately made to be inclusive of an entire *Series*) brought in an annual royalty of $1,000 to the Home Mission Board.

But the first Sunday School Board was not the first publishing venture of Southern Baptists. Even as early as 1846, at the first regular meeting of Southern Baptists following 1845, there was a committee to survey the need for other boards in addition to the Home and Foreign Boards which had been created in 1845. The Convention was especially interested in the possibility of a board of publication. This special committee concluded that the Convention should not "embarrass itself with any enterprise for the publication and sale of books."

Whereupon, aggressive and progressive Southern Baptists, not satisfied with this negative conclusion of the special committee, and independent of the Convention, but representing in its membership leading Southern Baptists, created the Southern Baptist Publication Society. This Society continued in operation, with headquarters in Charleston, South Carolina, as late as 1863. In these years the Society received more than $100,000 in gifts and published more than eighty different books, according to Homer L. Grice in the *Encyclopedia of Southern Baptists*. The first book published by the Society in 1849 was written by the Convention's second president, R. B. C. Howell, *The Way of Salvation*.

The Southern Baptist Publication Society also became embroiled in the Landmark issue. The prominent J. R. Graves made it a point to see that such embroilment came about. Graves attacked the Society's last secretary, J. P. Tustin, no doubt with some justification, indeed with strong warrant from the Landmark viewpoint. Graves charged Tustin with recognition of pedobaptist ministers. After Tustin resigned, he became an Episcopal priest. No doubt the Society which he had headed suffered from his leadership which was at odds with doctrines and practices of Southern Baptists.

The Society was independent of the Convention but supported in the main by Southern Baptists, as was implicit in its name. At the same time, the Convention had officially engaged before the Civil War in another kindred publication effort through what was known as the Bible Board, 1851-63. This Board was located in Nashville. That very location no doubt contributed to the bitter controversy which developed between the Bible Board personnel and the Landmark movement, represented in the tempestuous career of J. R. Graves. This Board was set up by the Convention for colportage, Sunday School, and Bible work.

Not only was it beset with the destructive Landmark involvement brought to great intensity in the Howell-Graves strife, but, as was true of all other religious work at the time, it was caught in the devastation of the Civil War. Finally, the existence of the Bible Board as an operating agency became problematic with the capture of Nashville by the Federal army in 1862. Officially this Board was dissolved by the Convention in 1863, although its final report to the Convention came in 1866, after the war. During its ten years the Bible Board worked with local and state colportage and with state Bible societies.

"What it experienced," writes Homer L. Grice in the *Encyclopedia of Southern Baptists,* "was a part of the painful and often costly efforts Southern Baptists had to make through many years in order to develop a cohesive and effective denomination."

Still one other publishing venture is in the background, that of the so-called Southern Baptist Sunday School Union, 1857-62. From the outset, this union was in large measure the child of two leading Landmarkers, J. R. Graves and A. C. Dayton. Dayton had been the corresponding secretary of the Bible Board, but in an embroilment of the Board, provoked by R. B. C. Howell and other Convention persons, had been forced out of office, after which Graves projected his brainchild, the Southern Baptist Sunday School Union. R. B. C. Howell, the Convention president and a pastor in Nashville, would give no personal endorsement to the Union but rather criticized it sharply as being the personal exploitation of J. R. Graves. Howell charged that Graves was attempting to control the promotion of Southern Baptist Sunday School work and to capture the publications for the Sunday Schools. The abortive Union became a casualty of these controversies.

As a summary of these complex, interrelated, and usually controversial efforts, Homer L. Grice writes in the *Encyclopedia of Southern Baptists:* "The successive failures of the Southern Baptist Publication Society . . . the Sunday School Union, and the Sunday School Board . . . developed a defeatist attitude which prevailed among Southern Baptists for many years and which discouraged organized Sunday school and publication work. The American Baptist Publication Society entered the vacant field and became so entrenched that Southern Baptists did not again authorize a Sunday School Board until May, 1891. Even then they provided no funds for their venture."

That conclusion of the researcher is a valid appraisal. It helps one to understand the opposition to Frost's proposal which now becomes the subject of the next chapter.

4

Into the Heart of the Conflict

A more unlikely candidate to lead in establishing a denominational publishing board could scarcely be found than J. M. Frost. In his own personal account of the launching of the Board, Frost writes in *The Sunday School Board, Its History and Work:* "A new question was brought into the discussion, the question of the Convention creating a new Board to have charge specifically of these publications and to look otherwise after the interests of the Sunday School cause in our churches. This new question brought me into the very heart of the conflict that was on; indeed, the question of a new Board was of my making, and made the issue more sharp and concrete."

Frost's entry into the discussion is surprising. That he should have the audacity to propose a new Board is fairly startling.

That John A. Broadus and Basil Manly, Jr., should have assumed the initiative in the beginning of the first Board in 1863 is not only logical but entirely to be expected. Even as early as 1860, they were recognized spokesmen for biblical studies. Both were professors at the Southern Baptist Seminary then located in Greenville, South Carolina. They were recognized leaders in Convention affairs.

But J. M. Frost? Who was he? Certainly he was not then,

at forty-one years of age, an outspoken leader in Convention affairs. At that time in 1890 the longtime leader and recognized spokesman among Southern Baptists, John A. Broadus, had only five years ahead of him in his eventful career. Manly, too, had even then reached the near termination (just two years away) of his useful life.

A logical expectation for leadership in establishing a publishing board would have been a man like Lansing Burrows, secretary and statistician of the Convention. His popularity was well established. Indeed, he was first elected to the new Board's leadership after the Convention finally decided to establish it.

But, Frost? He was no denominational stalwart, nor had his voice ever been raised in discussion of the Sunday School question and its meaning to Southern Baptists.

At the recurring Convention sessions, when Sunday School publications had been the focus of lively interest for at least five years, 1885 to 1889, Frost had taken "no public part in the discussion, though deeply concerned." Neither had he been active in the Convention sessions, although "always present and earnest in my study of its affairs."

Of the recurring Convention discussions on the Sunday School issue, Frost asserts that the "severest of them all" was at Memphis in May 1889. Frost himself did not participate in that heated discussion. It is, therefore, more surprising that his own personal entry into the debate should have begun on an eventful night of the next January. Recalling twenty-five years later the beginning of his personal involvement, Frost insists that "my first thought of the new Board had no outside connection with any person or place so far as I can now recall or knew at the time. I crave the privilege of saying in the simplest way, God touched me and I thought it."

The way God touched him, Frost also relates in direct account, even stating in detail that he was "living in the parsonage on Libby Hill, at No. 5, Twenty-ninth Street." Frost recalls: "I was awakened from sleep with the thought of a new Board in full possession. . . . It worked itself out in a set of resolutions which I determined while lying there to present to the Fort Worth Convention. They were written out in the early morning light."

The resolutions, proposing a Board of Publications, were printed in the *Religious Herald* on February 27, 1890. Frost sent the proof sheets with a personal letter to the denominational papers in the South and also to the executive of the American Baptist Publication Society.

Who was this forty-one-year-old pastor to whom came at nighttime the conviction of the need for a publishing board? Why was he gripped with this strong urgency, which, even before rising from his sleepless bed, he was determined to offer as a resolution at the forthcoming Convention the next May in Fort Worth?

James Marion Frost was born in Georgetown, Kentucky, February 10, 1849, the son of a pastor. He attended Georgetown College, graduating therefrom in 1871. For health reasons he was not privileged to attend Southern Seminary, but entered the pastorate following his graduation from college. He had served two churches in Kentucky—Maysville, and what is now known as Calvary Church in Lexington. Then, at thirty-two, he had gone to Staunton, Virginia, to serve there until called to the prestigious First Baptist Church in Selma, Alabama, in 1884. After the 1889 Convention at Memphis, he had moved to Richmond to become pastor of the Leigh Street Baptist Church, which he served until he accepted the corresponding secretaryship of the new Sunday School Board in July 1891.

No doubt the most influential aspect of his entry into the discussion of a new publishing board had occurred at Selma when the persuasive Isaac Taylor Tichenor had first convinced Frost that Southern Baptists should "make their own literature." In that Selma congregation were the Haralsons and the Mallorys. A predecessor in the pastorate had been J. B. Hawthorne, perhaps the most eloquent of Southern Baptist preachers of that generation. At the Fort Worth Convention, now scheduled for May 1890, the president was the Convention's first layman presiding officer, Jonathan Haralson of Selma, who in response to the resolution Frost himself would offer, was called on to name the committee to consider Frost's proposal. Haralson was still presiding the next year in Birmingham when the committee was named to deal decisively with Frost's proposal. The Selma layman named two former pastors, J. B. Hawthorne and J. M. Frost, and his neighbor, H. S. D. Mallory, father of Miss Kathleen Mallory, later Woman's Missionary Union secretary. Thus, on this significant committee to consider the resolution looking toward a new board of publications were two Selma laymen and two former pastors of Selma, which caused Walter N. Jackson in his *History of the Selma Baptist Church of Christ,* to remark that the Selma church "had as much a hand in the creation of the new Board . . . as most any church anywhere."

Frost had offered his proposed resolutions of publications in the *Religious Herald* on the strength of the content of the proposal, and not as a recognized spokesman among Southern Baptists. It was in the parsonage of Leigh Street Church that "God touched me and I thought it."

Frost recalls that he signed his resolutions for publication on his forty-first birthday—February 10, 1890. Immediately, he says, his proposal "brought on the most vigorous discussion which we had yet had." Baptist papers of the South, "while saying kindly things, set themselves in opposition, . . . practically all the Baptist papers of the South were keeping a constant fire on that proposition for a new Board."

"It was," he relates, "a trying ordeal, and I twinge a bit even now as it is all recalled. . . . I maintained high regard for those opposing, wondered at my contravening their judgment and leadership, but was driven on with a conviction that could not yield. I wondered then, and wonder even to this day, as it comes back in memory."

Rising from the parsonage bed, Frost wrote these resolutions, which were published along with a supporting article in the *Religious Herald* for February 27, 1890:

"1. *Resolved,* That to the Boards already existing we add another, to be elected at this session of the Convention, and to be called the Board of Publication of the Southern Baptist Convention,

"2. *Resolved,* That this Board of Managers be elected as provided for in Art. V. of the Constitution, and located as may hereafter be determined,

"3. *Resolved,* That the Committee on Nominations besides nominating the Board of Managers be requested to recommend also the place of its location,

"4. *Resolved,* That the Sunday school literature, known as *Kind Words Series,* including all contracts with publishers, writers and others in the interest of its publication, be transferred from the Home Mission Board to the Board of Publication,

"5. *Resolved,* That it shall not be within the province of said Board to publish other literature than that committed to its care by these resolutions except such as may be necessary to the greater efficiency of the series, or as the Convention itself may hereafter direct,

"6. *Resolved,* That any profit accruing from said publications, after a liberal allowance for the conduct of its business, the Board of Managers shall appropriate as the Convention may order from time to time."

In exactly this same language, Frost offered these resolutions at the first afternoon session of the Convention in Fort Worth the following May. By Frost's motion the resolutions were referred to a committee composed of one representative from each state, the account of which committee's report will come in a later chapter. Now it is in order to look more definitely at Frost's supporting arguments which were published along with the proposed resolutions in the *Herald* for February 27, 1890.

In his article, Frost first disavowed any involvement in "the recent controversy" which by all accounts had wracked the Convention for at least five years, beginning in 1885 and reaching its peak of discord at the last session in 1889 in Memphis. He declared that he was concerned with the more fundamental issue of the disposition of the basic question of Sunday School literature, which was focused upon the disposition of the existing *Kind Words Series.*

"It seems to me a question of great moment," Frost wrote in the *Herald* article, "one that vitally concerns the interest of our Zion, and deserves earnest and careful consideration. I respectfully submit these resolutions as an answer to the question; and throw them out in the hope that discussion will either lead to their adoption or to the development of something better."

Then Frost made it clear that his intent was intended as no reflection on the Home Board, which then had the responsibility for the *Kind Words Series,* nor on the American Baptist Publication Society which at the time was supplying much, if not most, of the literature used in the

Sunday Schools of Southern Baptist churches.

He wanted it understood that his resolutions were not "born of sectionalism," although he readily granted his own Southern background and loyalty. Still he did not introduce these resolutions with any intent of hurting the American Baptist Publication Society, located in Philadelphia, but of introducing publication activity designed specifically for Southern churches. He even ventured the prediction that the new Board and the Society could both "increase the efficiency of each." So, he insisted that "in submitting these resolutions, I respectfully insist that they may be considered and discussed upon their own merits as a measure to meet demands that are upon us."

Coming more directly to the purpose of his resolutions, Frost wrote that they were intended to "perpetuate the *Kind Words Series,* and provide for making it more effective." There were, he insisted, "imperative reasons why the *Series* should be retained under the control of the Convention." This he had in mind in proposing the formation of a Board of Publications.

"The arguments which will set it aside will set aside the Convention itself; arguments which justify preserving the Convention in its integrity demand also the keeping of *Kind Words Series,* . . . it is no appeal to sectionalism. . . . The Southern Baptist Convention is a geographical necessity. It is founded upon the great principle which we apply in city work with city churches, in state work with district associations, and is equally applicable and effective when applied to national work. . . . The Baptists of America and of the world are stronger for having had the Southern Baptist Convention. Even our fathers built more wisely than they knew. I am for what will make the Convention more powerful and efficient in occupying its territory and making it a stronghold of truth."

With eloquent conviction Frost came to the heart of his argument for a board to produce Sunday School literature, a need which he said "grew out of tragic neglect. As things now go in the sessions of the Convention," he wrote, "the Sunday school work hardly gets even a recognition. This discovery, made in a recent study of the minutes, surprised me. We are doing almost nothing in an organic, united movement to foster this great interest.

"The Sunday school lies at the base of all missionary enterprises—indeed, is almost the basis of the future church at home and abroad. Its opportunities and possibilities are simply immense, but in the minutes of the last Convention, this department of Christian endeavor is almost conspicuous by its absence—even in the statistical tables. It is of sufficient importance to deserve, and has grown to sufficient magnitude to require, a separate management—a Board of Managers charged with supplying proper literature, and by wise methods increasing the number and power of the Sunday schools and bringing them in contact with the Convention by annual reports. No one can tell the immense outcome from such a management pushing this interest with agencies and forces such as are now at work for the Foreign Board and the Home Board."

The new Board, said Frost, even in his initial proposal, would accomplish far more than just through "supplying proper literature." While quickly granting that "the supplying of periodical literature as helps" was "of immense importance," it was in his mind even at the beginning "only one feature of the work, only one factor of the plan." There were, he said, "other things to be done, all looking to the advancement of the Sunday School interests. The present and the future demand a new agency charged with this special enterprise."

He saw the new Board, by supplying literature and lead-ing in the development of Sunday School work, to be at the base of the denomination's missionary purposes. He was convinced that "the present and the future demand a new agency charged with this special enterprise." Indeed from the time of his conviction in Richmond on that January night in 1890, Frost perceived a publication board as being as definitely supportive of missions as were the two mission boards themselves. This conviction he stated very definitely in his supporting article.

Frost therefore argued for his proposed board on the basis of its potential value to the denomination, in support of missions as well as being a self-sustaining financial operation. He pointed out that the *Kind Words Series* was a most valuable "property" of the Convention. It would be foolish to allow the *Series* by default to be lost to the Convention. Even at that time, he pointed out that the "*Kind Words Series* is worth $15,000." It was paying $1,000 a year into the treasury of the Home Board: "But everyone knows that this sum is below the real worth of the *Series*. Why throw it away? Why sell it even at a good price? We can increase its money value, and at the same time make it a power whose immense worth, as an effective agency, cannot be stated in dollars and cents."

With irresistible conviction, Frost asserted that "the fur-nishing of helps to our Sunday schools through a long term of years will exert an immeasurable influence in behalf of our missionary Boards and largely determine their standing in the distant future. The *Series* is, therefore, valuable as a denominational investment."

Frost concluded his argument by pointing out that the stopgap contract for the publication of the *Kind Words*

Series would expire in 1891. Thus, action should be taken at the forthcoming 1890 Convention to guarantee the continued operation of these publications as a Convention enterprise, and under the management of this proposed new board.

Frost's proposal came as a new voice in the issue of Sunday School publications. He initiated a new movement to establish a new board when he himself could do so with no background of prior Convention leadership or even active involvement. At the time he was not a towering figure among Southern Baptists such as had been the earlier two, Broadus and Manly, who had started the first Board.

He came to this role by his own initiation on the basis of conviction that he could not yield. It was indeed because God had impressed and he had thought it, not at all by reason of a demonstrative career experience. His proposal had to stand on its merit, and never by reason of the driving influence of a towering personality. It indeed was the projection of a conviction, planted in the young pastor's mind and soul at Selma, Alabama, through that conversation with the eloquent leader, Isaac Taylor Tichenor, who by the gatepost of his friend Haralson at midnight had insisted to the young pastor that Southern Baptists must "make their own literature."

It was this kind of logic and conviction that brought Frost to his leadership role in 1890. An unlikely candidate for leadership in creating a publishing Board? Yes—and also no. Yes, because the young new leader was not then established in the leadership role. And no, because he was inspired by a conviction which brought him from his sleepless slumber to engage from then even to the end of his days in a magnificent purpose.

This evaluation now is based on an earnest effort to assess

the man's likelihood at the particular junction in time for himself and for the Convention. Then, one would, of neces-sity, be forced to conclude that he was not a likely candidate for the leadership. Now, in retrospect, the student will assess his capacity for that leadership on the basis of the unfolding record. That record now is well known following his quarter of a century in the position created in the main by his own initiative. Certainly now one assesses his qualifications as being superlative for the particular task in which with remarkable success his labors were committed. But at that time, in 1890 and 1891, he was indeed an upstart coming to a strange and startling task unsuited by any objective assessment of his previous record, and even for which by background and training and experience he was obviously poorly qualified.

It is to this lack that he frankly refers when he speaks of twinging "a bit even now as it is all recalled." Now from this distance it is no surprise that he did wonder "at my contravening their judgment and leadership"—that is, the leadership of those who were the recognized stalwarts of his day. In the face of his own personal lack in experience and in comparison with the strong position of such men as John A. Broadus, J. B. Gambrell, Lansing Burrows, and Editor A. E. Dickinson of the *Religious Herald* he was truly "driven on with the conviction that could not yield."

As has been remarked earlier, he did not know at the time of the former Sunday School Board. When this infor-mation came to him by a letter and a newspaper clipping from a friend, he said, "I saw at once that without knowing it I had in my proposition only gathered up the broken threads of history as if knitting them together again. Mani-festly the unseen hand that touched the heart and mind in the nighttime was weaving the life plan for Southern

Baptists." That was his personal assessment of the meaning of the events into which his life was so strangely projected.

Writing later of the events, Frost declared that "the momentous issue . . . had almost become a threatening crisis in the affairs of our people. Those days of storm and stress in our denominational life can hardly be appreciated except by those who passed through them. And it is quite manifest now, looking back after a quarter of a century, that no one on either side of the conflict understood at the time the full meaning of that gigantic movement. . . . A great people were in the throes of 'growing pains,' were coming to their own in heritage and responsibility. God was leading them a way they had not gone hitherto, and bringing them to the kingdom for larger service in the hour of need and opportunity."

It was conviction like this that held Frost steadily to his accepted and personally initiated task.

The surprising and immediate opposition provoked by his proposal will be detailed in the next chapter.

5

The Instant Opposition

The proposal by J. M. Frost to create a board of publication, as published in the *Religious Herald* on February 27, 1890, was "intended in spirit and purpose as a compromise measure." But, it "brought on the most vigorous discussion which we had yet had."

The vigor of that discussion is really not surprising in view of the background as traced by Frost himself with deft and precise strokes. The importance of Sunday School literature and of a full Sunday School enterprise made the proposal one of the very chief questions confronting a religious body.

As earlier indicated, Frost did not know when he came to the conviction of offering his resolutions that there had been an earlier Sunday School Board, 1863-1873. When finally, after a decade of frustration and mounting debts, that first Board was discontinued, its liabilities and potentials were assigned to the Home Mission Board. Strangely this combining of Home Missions with Sunday School publications became an aggravation of an already existing publication problem. That assignment of double functions to the Home Board carried responsibility for the existing Sunday School paper, *Kind Words*. Moreover, the aggravation of the problem with regard to this Sunday School paper and other proposed papers, grew apace in the 1870s under the Home Board management.

One very definite personal aspect was the overpowering influence of Isaac Taylor Tichenor, secretary of the Home Mission Board. "No one surpassed him," says Frost, "as dreamer of dreams and seer of visions in denominational needs and power of conquest, and not many equaled him in making others through his eloquence on the platform see what he saw and believe what he believed."

It was this very kind of eloquence which first convinced J. M. Frost as a young pastor in Selma to perceive the need of Southern Baptists to "make their own literature." That Tichenor had done in his midnight tryst with Frost at the gatepost of their mutual friend, Hugh Haralson, in Selma back in 1889.

Perhaps with similar force Tichenor had persuaded Southern Baptists. Again and again his Home Mission Board reports and recommendations called on Southern Baptists to enlarge the Sunday School publications then under the direction of Tichenor's Board. Frost points out that this had been done repeatedly in the Conventions of 1885 in Mobile; in Montgomery the following year, 1886; in Louisville, 1887; in Richmond, 1888; and in Memphis in 1889. Each successive year the vexing problem of what to do about Sunday School publications had claimed the attention of Southern Baptists with characteristic Tichenor fervor, until, as Frost remarks, "at Memphis the severest of them all."

Almost certainly Tichenor, in these recurring appeals for the enlargement of the *Kind Words Series*, had overpersuaded Southern Baptists. His fervent eloquence moved them to adopt the recommendations offered in the Home Board reports, but there was still a restiveness about these Home Board aggressions. There were subtle, maybe even subconscious, reactions to the eloquent persuasiveness of their leader.

At any rate, and very likely as a typical example of popular reaction, Frost states that the *Religious Herald* in Virginia "had been adverse to the Home Board movement, and became adverse, also, to my proposition for a new board." In those years of the 1880s the opposition to the recurring appeals for enlargement of publications became more and more severe, "becoming at times almost a war on the Home Mission Board in every department of its work." This opposition, he makes clear, was related to Tichenor's strong appeals for enlargement of the Sunday School publications. He says that "Dr. Tichenor believed in the movement profoundly, even unto conviction, and walked the heights in his vision of what these periodicals were worth for the onward movement of our cause."

"But over against it all," writes Frost, "with heroism and generalship equal to the task, Dr. Tichenor and his splendid array of able associates and supporters held on their way with slow but steady advance. They carried the issue successively and successfully through sessions of the Convention." It was Tichenor's leadership which first brought the Convention to consider the Sunday School publications matter at the sessions in Augusta in 1885. A year later at Montgomery the Home Board was authorized to publish a series of Sunday School helps—"provided no indebtedness should be incurred." Although the vote in the successive sessions was affirmative, the restlessness and later indecision continued. By 1889, according to Frost, Baptists of the South were "profoundly stirred from Maryland to Texas."

Also significant in the background was the prominent place of the American Baptist Publication Society of Philadelphia, "with immense assets and resources" and with "many earnest friends in the South." This Society, Frost recounts, was offering "creditable periodicals and employing many southern writers." It had "large patronage among our churches, and gathered large harvests in return from its business." Frost admits that it did "no little benevolent work among our people, and had come to hold a high and strong place with many." He says that this vantage ground could not be "stated too strongly," even to the point of using its established influence and "all the forces at its command" to withstand "the Home Board movement." The Society even claimed to have "preempted the field" and therefore it "challenged the right of the Convention to publish Sunday school periodicals."

These, in brief, occasioned the immediate opposition to Frost's proposal for a board of publication. Moreover, the discussion which followed grew out of a current acknowledgment of the significance of the issue. Sunday Schools in the churches then were essentially a project for children. But even so, no one discounted the potential value of literature aimed at helping to an understanding of God's Word.

Thoughts about publications recurringly turned primarily toward catechisms for children—basic questions with primary answers. A contract for one such catechism to be written by John A. Broadus would be made in 1891, with a second also in the planning stage. These helps were universally regarded to be of fundamental worth and significance to the understanding by children of God's revelation. There was no failure to appreciate the importance of such publications. That was sufficient reason for the immediate and voluminous attention given to Frost's proposal for a new board of publication.

One example of that recognized significance is the space given by the *Religious Herald* to Frost's article and immediate comment. The first article by Frost, containing his proposals, occupied two columns on the first page of the *Herald* (February 27, 1890). A column in the *Herald* was a full twenty-seven inches. Two columns would accommodate more than 2,300 words.

In addition to that lengthy discussion by the Richmond pastor, the *Herald*, in the same issue, carried over a column in editorial comment opposing the proposal—a total of 1,600 words by the editor. Altogether, in the Frost article and the editorial, the *Herald* published more than three full columns, a total of around 4,000 words in a single issue.

The *Herald* invited comments on Frost's proposal. Three weeks later, its editorial page was devoted to "all the communications which we have received touching the proposition of Dr. Frost to create and maintain a Southern Publication Board." The introductory paragraph and the nine letters that had been received covered three and a half columns in the *Herald*—a total of over 3,000 words. Thus, in its two issues of February 27 and March 20, the *Herald* devoted some six and a half columns, 7,000 words, to the discussion. Other papers gave similar attention to the matter.

Seven of the *Herald* letters were in opposition. Only two favored the Frost proposal.

"The post of honor" (first letter in the nine) was given by the editor to the "Old Shepherd," the always vocal J. W. M. Williams of Baltimore. Ever ready to speak his mind, the Maryland pastor asserted that there was no need for such a board, since the American Baptist Publication Society fully and satisfactorily supplied the needed literature. A new publishing house would inevitably provoke competition: "As conscientious businessmen, the officers of the ABP Society will feel compelled to push their publications." The officers of our "Board of Publication" will feel the same obligation. "The weaker," Williams wrote, "must finally go under. Then there would be bitter feelings at the grave of the departed." Williams argued that the matter should be kept out of the Convention while they concentrated "our prayers and our business, and our efforts, and our money, to sustain the Convention by supporting the Home and Foreign Boards." He felt that the one organization needed to supply religious literature was the American Baptist Publication Society.

"I am afraid," Williams concluded, "there will be no peace, even among ourselves, so long as the question of Sunday school literature is discussed at every meeting of our Convention."

A variation from the tone of opposition was expressed by W. F. Dunaway (address not given) who wrote plainly, "I will record myself as favorable to the contemplated movement."

This he did first on the ground that the Home Mission Board should be "relieved of the embarrassing work of publication. It has already received detriment enough from this source." Further, he asserted that there was "an irrepressible demand for a Southern Publication Society," which demand would never cease until the publication interests were given to a Southern agency.

Moreover, he insisted that such a movement was "a condition of peace" between "the Baptists of the North and the Baptists of the South." The establishment of their own publishing agency, Dunaway contended, was in the "interest and efficiency of the Southern Baptist Convention." He said that "this is the only body in the world, so far as I know, that commits the suicidal policy of entrusting its publications to a rival organization." The convinced Dunaway insisted that to make the Philadelphia Society "national is the entering wedge of our dissolution." He even asked if the Society had ever been of help to the Home and Foreign Mission Boards. Southern organizations, he said, were incomplete because they lacked a publication agency to advance the interest of the boards of missions.

On the other hand, the *Herald* editor pointedly rejected Frost's implication that a strong publication program was directly related to the preservation of the Convention. In his parallel comment the editor scoffed at that implication. "The integrity of the Southern Convention," wrote the editor, "is not in the remotest degree dependent upon the establishment and maintenance of a Publication Board." He was surprised that Frost "should, seemingly at least, take this ground."

The editorial then quoted from Frost's article: "The arguments which will set it [this separate publication business] aside will set aside the Convention itself; the arguments which justify preserving the Convention in its integrity demand also the keeping of *Kind Words* series."

The editor made no pretense of withholding his scorn. "It is a pity," he chided, "that so wise and judicious an article should be marred by such an untenable and inconsiderate proposition. The Convention existed in its integrity before such a series was born, and its birth or death has nothing to do with preserving or destroying it."

E. W. Winfrey, pastor in Culpepper, Virginia, proposed the appointment of a special committee "for a whole year's discussion and consideration." He was sure that "Fort Worth is not the place—1890 is not the time for the final settlement of this matter."

A relief from the consistent commendation of the existing Philadelphia Society was the suggestion in three of the letters that a separate independent private publisher be set up to offer Sunday School literature. Those who wanted other Sunday School helps could thus "do what they want done," said T. A. Reid of Crossroads, Maryland. Thereby the "Convention would forever be relieved of this troublesome question."

Of the nine letters published in the *Herald*, the most comprehensive was by "an eminent Georgia Lawyer," Alvan D. Freeman of Newnan, who proposed that the *Kind Words Series* be sold or given to the American Baptist Publication Society.

With convincing legalistic logic, Freeman had concluded that it was in the best interest of the Baptists of the whole country to support only one publishing house.

Kind Words, said Freeman, was born of strife and dissension. The papers had served "their day and purpose." The reasons for their existence had ceased, and they should "cease to live."

To sustain only one publishing agency, said Freeman, would be less expensive. Its increased earnings would be used to good purpose by the Society, as demonstrated in its benevolent record. Moreover, Freeman pointed out, the Society was much stronger to supply benevolent resources to the churches than would be a new publication board.

"Who," he asked, "can help poor schools? Who can give books and Bibles and literature by thousands to those who cannot buy? We have never done it, and cannot do it now. Who will do it if the Society is driven out while we are making the arrangements? For us to insist that the Society shall discontinue to do its great work here is to be like the boy who was not able to jump into the river and save his drowning brother, yet would not consent for anyone else to do it, for the reason that it was his duty to do it. We cannot relieve the religious destitution here, and shall we through pride or pride of opinion, hold back the money which is ready and able to do it, and witness the eternal undoing of men and women."

Freeman, in an apologetic note, said that he wrote at length because it was doubtful that he could attend the Convention the following May in Fort Worth.

One bright spot in the sheaf of letters in the *Herald* was the note from G. S. Anderson of Fort Deposit, Alabama, who said that the resolutions "are a God-send, and in their purpose and plan meet the direst necessity ever felt by Southern Baptists."

In summing up his recollection more than twenty years later of the editorial comments, Frost could recall only two state Baptist papers that consistently supported the resolutions—*The Baptist and Reflector* of Tennessee and *The Western Recorder* of Kentucky. "So," Frost wrote, "the line-up was made and the discussion increased in vigor as the weeks passed."

In his recall of the much discussion, Frost evidently momentarily forgot the commendation in *The Alabama Baptist*, and the action of the Georgia Baptist Convention endorsing the resolutions. Later he did remember and recorded that the Baptists of Georgia at their meeting in April, which was the only state convention holding its sessions in the spring, after "a discussion, able, earnest, and prolonged," voted for the new board and sent a memorial to that effect to the Fort Worth Convention.

The letters in the *Herald* were typical of comments in all of the Baptist papers in the South. Thus Frost recalled that "things were shaping and lines being drawn for the issue in the approaching sessions of the Southern Baptist Convention." Throughout the whole South, "from Maryland to Texas the Baptists were stirred with the issue, surging almost as the sea surges."

The unusual means by which they made their plans to move on to Fort Worth will be detailed in the next chapter, "All Aboard for Fort Worth."

6

All Aboard for Fort Worth

Two topics claimed the attention of Baptists in the South in the spring of 1890. The first was, of course, the principal issue of what to do about Sunday School publications in response to the proposed resolutions by J. M. Frost of Richmond.

The second was really incidental—how to reach Fort Worth in May for the annual meeting of the Southern Baptist Convention. At these sessions the momentous proposal of J. M. Frost to establish a board of publications would be thrashed out in all of its many faceted aspects.

The ultimate decisions on getting to Fort Worth became a human commentary on life of the times and on modes of transportation. Before many weeks of that spring had passed, a unique experience was prominently in the offing: Southern Baptists for the first time in their history would ride their own Baptist train. Indeed, before the time to embark on their momentous journey there had been arranged not just one, but at least two, special Baptist trains.

By the beginning of the last decade of the twentieth century railroading in America had completed its great expansion to the entire breadth of the continent. Commodore Vanderbilt and his peers had done their work. The nation was embraced by steel rails reaching from one ocean

to the other. Railroading had now by reason of these con-
joining lines become the industry of a still burgeoning nation.
No longer was commerce primarily dependent on the emotional ties between the newly developed continent and the
nations abroad. It was domestic transportation that filled
the tills of a nation's markets. Railroading was the industry.
While being significant for the transport of food and materials, railroading was also the means of human transportation.
Water routes had faded from their earlier popularity as
modes of travel. It was now the steam engines with their
palace carriages that appealed to the footloose and travel
enthusiasts. The beckoning regions, while still partially ac-
cessible by river and canal and by Conestoga and covered
wagon, were to be reached primarily along these gleaming
steel bands which spanned the continent.

It was therefore a development of the times which
brought about the first Baptist special train to a Southern
Baptist Convention. There is also romantic logic in the
circumstance that the first Baptist special brought the messengers to the bustling new Western city. Baptists twice
before had gone to the Lone Star state, in 1874 at Jefferson
when only 222 measured the slim crowd, and at Waco in
1883 when 612 messengers were registered. But now in 1890
it was a different story, as they were to move on Fort Worth
with their first, and even perhaps at the same time their
second, special Baptist train.

Significance also is to be found in the primary issue to
be debated in those sessions. Every possible angle must be
surveyed as to whether Southern Baptists should "make their
own literature." This was the issue, definite, comprehensive,
even as railroading had become the economic industry of
the continent. Railroading was the means of getting there,
and the issue of publications was the big question that

brought them there in record numbers.

It had not been long—just forty-five years—since R. B. C. Howell of Nashville had complained in 1845 that a hastily called meeting in Augusta, Georgia, to consider organizing Baptists of the South was ill-advised on the ground that representatives from Tennessee could not be expected at a moment's notice to make the trip by horseback of some four or five hundred miles. Horseback, carriage, and riverboat had been principal means of travel less than half a century before the upcoming 1890 meeting in Fort Worth. But these slow and tedious modes of travel were no longer in the thinking of Baptists by 1890.

In that setting the railroads made good capital of their transportation business. There was no lack of their zeal to bring messengers to the annual Convention in Fort Worth. Through the months of March and April, and even to the very beginning of May, the Baptists papers were bombarded with train schedules, early, tentative, and final reports about "solid special trains," and warnings to messengers not to be misled by the announcements of competing lines.

There were then three principal routes from the Southeast to Fort Worth. One was the direct journey straight from Atlanta, across Alabama to Meridian, across the river at Vicksburg, on by Shreveport, and finally to Fort Worth. There was also the northern passage through Chattanooga, to Nashville, Memphis, Little Rock, and the Texas destination. The crescent route beginning also in Atlanta, carried the messengers to Mobile, along the spectacular Gulf Coast, through the sugar and cotton plantations of Louisiana, on to Houston, and then across the broad prairies into Fort Worth.

A route through the mid area, advertised as the shortest, the most direct and least time consuming—only thirty-six hours from Atlanta, and involving only one night en route—was first advertised as "the Baptist special." Then a competing line advertised "The True Baptist Special" by way of New Orleans with its spectacular scenery along the coast and the "vernal splendor" of Louisiana.

The second had logical reason for its claim as the "True Special." The plans had been made, approved, and promoted by the secretaries of the Convention, Lansing Burrows of Augusta, Georgia, and O. F. Gregory of Baltimore. This "True Special" originated in Baltimore and Richmond with a car filled with messengers from Maryland and Virginia. It proceeded through North Carolina, adding coaches as needed to accommodate additional messengers, on through South Carolina, and was joined in Atlanta with coaches as required for Georgia messengers. In Montgomery other cars were added from Birmingham, Tennessee, and Kentucky, so that the "solid" train continued on its way to Mobile and New Orleans.

Recognizing the competitive spirit of the rail lines, *The Christian Index* in the weeks of preparation pointed out that "there are more ways than one" to reach Fort Worth. "There are different routes, all of them good perhaps, and messengers can take choice and blame only themselves if they fail to go on the best road. The *Index* will vote a split ticket in this election of routes. One will cross the river at New Orleans and he will get a whiff of the sea breezes and quaff the magnolia. The other, Dr. Nunally [an editor], will cross the river at Vicksburg, taking the shortest line by several hundred miles, get the benefit of the northern breezes and the balmy gulf breezes and save six hours of time."

The coaches were described as Palace sleeping cars, with reclining seats in the chair cars, either of which, according to the passenger's wish and purchase, could be occupied without change from Atlanta to Fort Worth on either route. One paper stated that the equipment being made available by the railroads was the same as used by the "Texas delegation two years ago to Richmond" when the Convention met in the Virginia city.

A note in *The Western Recorder* of Kentucky gave more practical details. One car had been reserved to operate out of Louisville at a total cost of $150. Its twenty-four berths were available at $6.25 each, but the editor made it clear that every berth must be taken if the special car was to make its run. The round trip fare from Louisville to Fort Worth was $26.35; from Cincinnati, $28.30; from Nashville, $21.75. That car would run the crescent route by Nashville, Montgomery, Mobile, and New Orleans which was "the best route all things considered." It would join the group of brethren from Maryland, Virginia, North Carolina, South Carolina, Georgia, and Alabama at Montgomery.

"We are able to announce the complete details of this pleasant enterprise," announced *The Christian Index* for April 17, 1890. "The idea is the outgrowth of the minds of several brethren in different portions of the country, and has been pursued in the interest of the brethren and not of any particular line of railway. . . . While there are several ways of getting to Fort Worth, investigation proved that the one selected had peculiar merits, it being finely constructed with steel rails and excellent roadbeds, and passing through sections of country that is fraught with great interest. Consequently agreement was reached upon the line passing down through the cities of Mobile and New Orleans, along the beautiful Gulf Coast, and thence through the Teche country of Louisiana, with its attractive sugar plantations, and thence from the city of Houston up through the prairie country of Texas, which will then be bright in its vernal glory. The superior character of this line [will] enable the adoption of a time schedule which is remarkably fast, making the journey about 36 hours from Atlanta.

"The solid train of Pullman Palace cars, five or six in number, with reclining chair cars for those who do not care for the sleepers, will make a noteworthy event in the history of Southern Baptists, the first of its kind attempted among us.

"It will be better for the brethren," *The Index* urged, "to make themselves secure, by speaking for berths or chairs in this Train and not take the risk of being crowded unduly."

In another editorial comment, *The Index* expressed delight in the "plan to combine the brethren into a train of their own in which they can journey in common fellowship to their place of meeting."

In North Carolina, C. Durham, corresponding secretary, assured his readers that "it will be much more pleasant for us if all the North Carolina delegates and visitors shall go by the same route and the same train." He added that they had the names of twenty-seven "brethren and sisters who expect to go to Fort Worth." He encouraged others who wanted him to complete arrangements for them to advise immediately of their desire.

The Committee on Hospitality in Fort Worth cautioned through the state Baptist papers that arrangements were being made to accommodate "delegates only." Visitors, including wives and children of messengers, would not be entertained in the homes. These visitors, the committee pointed out, would have to find accommodations in hotels, a list of which was given with rates from $2.50 down to $1.00.

"Only delegates" did not include women. At an earlier

convention this question had been resolved when with the Arkansas delegation to the Convention in Augusta in 1885 there were two women present. The Convention quickly appointed a committee of five to deal with this serious problem and to make recommendation with reference to seating women as bona fide messengers to the Convention. Three on the committee recommended that they be seated, to the consternation of the Convention generally which ultimately sustained the minority report by a vote of 202 to 212, whereupon the women, not being officially seated, withdrew and thus averted a controversy. In that 1885 discussion, nine messengers had spoken in favor of seating the two Arkansas women, and six had spoken against it—all of this speaking resulting in turning the two women messengers away.

Thus in consistency with Convention policy, the Fort Worth Committee on Hospitality made arrangements to accommodate messengers only.

Evidently the warning from Fort Worth that only messengers would be entertained cast no apprehension in the minds of a number of messengers, who were favored on the journey with the presence of their wives. One of the intrepid women was a wife to no man, never would be—Annie Walker Armstrong of Baltimore, in the company all the way from her city of Baltimore across half the continent to Fort Worth.

Consternation among Baptists in the Southeast came with the news of flooding up and down the Mississippi. There were reports that trains could not operate on schedule and indeed that the lines might not be able to accommodate the crowds of travelers. These rumors caused the rail lines to issue the assurance that trains were operating on schedule, that they were not being unduly delayed by flooding, and that the roads would take care of all the business the Baptists expected to give them.

In spite of this assurance the Baptist trains were delayed, the one by New Orleans reaching Fort Worth nine hours late, while another was reported to be seventeen hours behind schedule.

Almost certainly there were reasons other than flooding for delay. The train through New Orleans stopped for "nearly one day" in order to give all a chance to see the city and to receive a generous welcome from "the brethren of the city on our return." This return stopover was in response to plans made by Baptists in New Orleans to welcome the travelers.

There was still another cause for change of plans. The Fort Worth Committee on Hospitality received word that some messengers were expecting to arrive in Fort Worth on May 7. The Hospitality Committee advised that there would be no accommodations for messengers that early: "*Do not* arrive here before the morning of the 8th. We have made no arrangements for anyone sooner than that," wrote the chairman of the Hospitality Committee plainly and bluntly. "No one here is expecting to entertain until the 8th and so you must not come until the 8th."

On Thursday, May 8, the trains arrived in the host city.

The editor of *The Religious Herald* sent this account to his paper: "We came into this booming western city at 6:00 P.M. on Thursday. We were nine hours late, but were consoled when we learned that the other trains were late also, one of them coming in seventeen hours behind time, and there were rumors that yet another was somewhere in the wilderness still. A somewhat better form of consolation was administered in the feast spread for our delighted eyes as we swept on through the boundless fields of Texas."

Reaching Fort Worth, he said there was "the usual inevitable pressure and confusion in arranging for the entertainment of delegates, but all things considered it was managed with expedition."

The Herald editor reported that "a brother has figured up what he thinks this Convention has cost, traveling expenses, etc. He makes it $45,000 and asks: 'Is it worth all that?' "

The editor of the *Biblical Recorder* (North Carolina) reported that "the True Baptist Special arrived safely at Fort Worth with over 400 persons to attend the Southern Baptist Convention. The journey from Raleigh, North Carolina, to Texas has been in many respects an exceedingly pleasant one, including good company, interesting scenes, and the best of attention by railroad officials."

Atlanta, he said, "fully deserves the good account given of her wonderful progress." The residences he reported to be "truly palatial," thrift, energy and haste being displayed on every hand.

A few hours ride beyond Atlanta brought the messengers to "the coke-ovens of Birmingham," which he said were the "wonder of the South." At Vicksburg it was noted that the Mississippi "had broken loose, flooding the country." Crossing "the father of waters, we found it not so easy and swift traveling as heretofore, and for a number of miles the train proceeded with great caution. We traveled," he reported, "with water on either side, whole vast plantations were literally submerged, houses deserted, and families carried away to the uplands."

The Christian Index reported that "the Baptist special train was a decided success." En route the travelers by a committee resolution expressed appreciation to those who had made the arrangements, including train officials and the Convention secretaries, Burrows and Gregory. In a sustained similar feeling the group, as they traveled away from Fort Worth, again expressed their thanks to the same men "for their unrivaled generalship."

In recalling that generalship, the *Biblical Recorder* editor remarked: "Lansing Burrows is in many respects a model Secretary. He is always at his post, prompt in the discharge of business, and seems to know everybody and almost everything about the Convention. Some have thought that he would lose nothing worth retaining by being less dictatorial in his manners. He means nothing by it, but still it is annoying to his brethren."

Very certainly this was a price paid by the efficient Convention secretary both in filling his official position and also in the incidental task of making plans for the messengers to have suitable means of transportation to and from the Convention sessions. It was one of the human factors in Convention service.

The human element became even more apparent the next year in Birmingham in a big debate on where the Convention would next meet. From Baltimore came an invitation, with the provision that messengers and visitors would personally bear the expenses of their entertainment. The invitation was definitely geared to a change in Convention policy, which from the beginning had seen the host city provide full entertainment for messengers. Now it was proposed that messengers also, along with wives and other visitors, should pay for their lodging and meals. One reporter suggested that this occasioned a livelier discussion than the big issue of what to do about Sunday School publications which had claimed primary attention year after year for almost a decade. Ultimately, at the 1891 session in Birmingham, it was voted to accept the invitation of Atlanta, rather than the one from Baltimore, because in Atlanta messengers would again be entertained.

But the discussion in 1891 had become so lively as to this practice of entertaining messengers, that the host pastor from the 1890 Fort Worth session was called on for an explanation. He said in Fort Worth there had been room enough and to spare to entertain all messengers and that when the Convention adjourned there still remained $450 in the hospitality treasury.

In the booming Western town of Fort Worth the Baptist delegations assembled "where the west begins" with its 1890 population of 23,000. The Virginia messengers had left their capital city, then boasting 81,000 inhabitants. Coming through his native Kentucky, Frost had changed trains in Lousiville, with 161,000 population. The progressive and bustling city of Atlanta in Georgia had 65,000. In "The Magic City" of Birmingham was an industrial complex of 26,000. The older Cresent City on the banks of the Mississippi in Louisiana claimed 242,000.

Among those who had been entertained in the host city of Fort Worth in 1890 was J. M. Frost, ready with his proposed resolutions for a board of publication. But Frost himself had not traveled one of the special trains. At the depot in Louisville he met one of his longtime friends who had not intended to attend the Convention, but at length was persuaded by his wife to go, since, as she said, "Brother Jimmy Frost may need you." Since the Virginia delegation had gone down from Richmond through the Carolinas to Atlanta and then on to New Orleans, it is rather safely assumed that Frost was not with them. Of course, it could be that he did join them by train from Louisville down in Montgomery, as did the Kentucky and Tennessee messengers. But rather it still may be surmised that he had determined to make the journey alone, rather than with the delegation from his state of Virginia, since he was in Louisville making a train connection.

Was it because he felt the intensity and overwhelming weight of opposition to his proposal that he decided not to go with his own state delegation? His own state paper, *The Religious Herald*, had been most vocal in opposition, even from February 27 when Frost's proposal was first published.

Or it may be that Frost simply came ahead of schedule into his native Kentucky to visit with home folks. This would afford some respite on the eventful journey to Fort Worth where he knew he would be engaged in a trying and dramatic exchange. He had reason for apprehension from the great swell of opposition which had been expressed in all of the state papers. At any rate, Frost appears to have been a lonely man en route to Fort Worth.

The question he had raised certainly had no want of interest. The editor of his own state paper asserted, "The one subject which towered above all others in popular interest at Fort Worth was the publication question."

Frost was ready at the first sounding of the president's gavel to introduce his proposal. The immediate and clear response to that proposition will next claim our interest.

7

Compromise in Texas

The editor of *The Religious Herald* was most certainly correct in reporting that "the one subject which towered above all others in popular interest at Fort Worth was the publication question." This was the surpassing topic in a Convention in which the attendance was so large that the *Herald* editor said "that the thoughtful members of the body seem impressed more and more with the necessity for reducing the representatives in some way." This proposal to reduce the size of the Convention was made more than once—in a year when the total registration of messengers reached 781, the largest ever to attend the Convention, except for the 835 in Richmond in 1888. This appeal of the Virginia editor was made in a year when the meeting was some 1,700 miles from Richmond.

Yet the attendance was so great that the delegates filled the beautiful auditorium of the First Baptist Church in Fort Worth and crowded the gallery. The crowds that filled the meeting place made the Virginia editor feel that a reduction in representation was a necessity.

But his disturbance was not only with the crowds that taxed the beautiful and spacious building. He was more concerned about representation. The Virginia editor pointed out that a casual survey showed that the Convention in

Fort Worth was dominated by messengers from such states as Texas, Arkansas, and Georgia, each of which filled its quota of representation, while Virginia entitled to 121 messengers had no more than thirty-two or thirty-three. Maryland, entitled to thirty-eight messengers, had only five. He said that the Convention was controlled by states like Texas, Arkansas, Georgia, Kentucky, and Mississippi. Both Georgia and Kentucky had their full quota.

On the principal issue to claim the attention of the messengers, the editor of *The Alabama Baptist* had written as early as March 13, 1890, that "the new movement to create a board of publication . . . is a matter of grave import." The Alabama editor appreciated "the frankness and fairness of J. M. Frost" who had announced in advance "his purpose to submit his proposal to the Convention in Fort Worth."

In that same vein, the *Biblical Recorder* (N.C.) said that Frost had "made for himself a host of friends who admire his sterling Christian character, his courage, and his tender and loving heart." He had introduced the proposal on which "the feeling of the Convention was intense" and to which the messengers looked forward as "the event of the Convention."

With remarkable determination J. M. Frost fulfilled his announced purpose, which he had made privately to himself on the night in January in Richmond. He allowed no loss of time in Fort Worth. As soon as the Convention had organized and was ready for business, Frost offered his resolutions word for word, just as he had written them before dawn in his Richmond parsonage that January night. His prompt action was moved by a conviction that he could not surrender.

There were also other resolutions offered immediately with reference to publications, including the one which the

Georgia Convention in April had ordered to be forwarded to the Southern Baptist Convention when it assembled at Fort Worth.

Upon motion of J. M. Frost, his resolutions were referred to a special committee of one from each state in the Convention. The Georgia resolutions were also referred to the same committee. Thus, consideration by the Convention at Fort Worth in 1890 was no simple matter involving simply one set of resolutions. There were more than those offered by Frost.

This issue of the publication of Sunday School literature brought on the scene many interrelated personalities. Call the roll of those who were involved, directly or indirectly: J. M. Frost, named as chairman of the special committee; J. B. Gambrell, who even in Fort Worth became the spokesman for the opposition. In addition were men like J. B. Hawthorne, C. C. Bitting, Isaac Taylor Tichenor, John A. Broadus, J. R. Graves, T. C. Teasdale, E. C. Dargan, J. H. Kilpatrick, B. H. Carroll, and Joshua Levering.

The above list is in no wise complete. Really, it is endless. The issue of Sunday School publications involved the entire Convention, past and present, men of renown as well as the unknown, leaders and would-be leaders. All were involved in that momentous setting—laymen and pastors, messengers and visitors. The whole gamut of Southern Baptist life came into significant focus to reach a measured conclusion.

Actually, the Convention came to no definite position in Fort Worth. All it could do in that welter of complexities was to arrive at a mutually and temporarily accepted compromise. The issue was too big, the involved personal interests were too inclusive to come to an answer at that one annual session.

One will withdraw from that overwhelming personality listing, though even it is incomplete. From a quick summary report how can one gain an understanding of the involvement of so many people, from such divergent backgrounds, each bringing his own distinctive viewpoint? It is staggering. It is impossible.

Why not simply set the two protagonists each in his respective place into that whirlpool? This plan of reporting would bring into the center the two principal participants, J. M. Frost and the commoner editor from Mississippi, J. B. Gambrell. These two represent the different views. One could with a degree of accuracy and satisfaction limit the report to the involvement and the viewpoints of these two. But there are other personalities to be considered.

There was, for instance, J. B. Hawthorne, eloquent and fervent pastor in Atlanta. Hawthorne was the kind of man who appears in every generation, the one with superlative talent in such compressed measure that every pastorless church at once wants to engage his services. Also, he was able to listen to many different calls. Now at fifty-three, this native of Alabama had served at least ten strong churches, some of them among the most prominent in the entire land. After studying law and then entering the ministry, he had been pastor in his home community in Alabama, then in Mobile, followed by a youthful tenure as a chaplain in the Confederate Army. He was pastor in Selma; Franklin Square in Baltimore; in Albany, New York, and also at Tabernacle in New York City; of Broadway Church in Louisville; at the First Baptist churches in Montgomery, Richmond, and Atlanta. Following his Atlanta ministry, Hawthorne was to be with the First Baptist Church of Nashville, and finally in Grove Avenue in Richmond.

A man with amazing qualities of attractive leadership,

and also one with roving feet, was this most eloquent and fervent preacher among Southern Baptists in 1890. Cathcart in his *Encyclopedia* describes the smooth-faced Hawthorne as being "tall, dignified, with commanding presence." He had great power as a speaker, with much dramatic skill.

A man as verbal as Hawthorne would most certainly be on his feet in the discussion of any significant issue. This he had done in his native Alabama, in Virginia, in New York State, in Maryland, and in Georgia. Indeed at the recent Georgia State Baptist Convention, held in Washington, Georgia, the previous April, Hawthorne was the chief spokesman to influence Georgia Baptists to adopt the resolution which by official instruction their secretary delivered to the Southern Baptist Convention in Fort Worth.

The speech Hawthorne had made in Washington, Georgia, he repeated in Fort Worth. It was marked by eloquence. It was also amazing in its recall of Southern Baptist history. Although himself no historian, but primarily a pulpiteer, Hawthorne had been strongly influenced by a man who even at the time of the Fort Worth meeting was pastor of the very church where earlier Hawthorne himself had served—Franklin Square in Baltimore. The pastor now in that Baltimore church was C. C. Bitting.

Who was Bitting? What part did he play, albeit indirectly, through Hawthorne's eloquence? Just this: Bitting, born in Philadelphia, and there baptized by J. L. Burrows, father of the better known Lansing Burrows, had in his earlier career been the corresponding secretary of the first Sunday School Board when it was located in Greenville, South Carolina. When that first Board was transferred to Memphis, Bitting elected to remain in South Carolina and soon became the district secretary for the South of the American Baptist Publication Society.

Bitting, therefore, was associated with Southern Baptist publication activity, both as the executive head of the first Sunday School Board and as the district representative of the Philadelphia Society when it moved into the vacuum to supply Southern Baptist churches Sunday School literature when their first Sunday School Board expired.

Now the effect of Bitting on Hawthorne's speech both in Washington, Georgia, and in Fort Worth: In his tenure with the Convention's first Sunday School Board, Bitting had stated very clearly and convincingly the reasons for a denomination to operate its own publishing enterprise. That statement had impressed Hawthorne, the man who in his multiple pastorates had once served the very church where now Bitting himself was the pastoral leader, Franklin Square in Baltimore.

But Bitting could not speak for himself either at the Georgia Convention or in Fort Worth, for he was sick abed in the parsonage in Baltimore. But, he did not need anyone to voice the position he had expressed twenty years earlier, if a man with the eloquence and fervency of Hawthorne was on hand to do it.

With one assent, Southern Baptist editors in 1890 said that Hawthorne made *the* speech at the Fort Worth Convention—the speech which did more than any other to influence the Convention's disposition of the Frost resolutions.

Quite frankly, Frost himself was not the kind to deliver a moving address. He did speak in his characteristic manner—incisively, earnestly, but he had no eloquence to match the fervency of the clean-shaven Hawthorne.

With convincing earnestness, Hawthorne summarized what Bitting had written in 1868: "These were the great reasons for our denomination to produce its own literature:

(1) supplies from external sources are never adapted to our wants; (2) they would never be received with the same confidence as would ours; (3) they give to others the control of our work; (4) publication from without removes the stimulus to production by our own competent authors; (5) such publications coming from a distant source sow discord among us; (6) with equal reason one could argue for destroying the Convention itself as to destroy the Convention publishing activites; (7) we can never be really represented in these societies of the north."

Beyond this, Hawthorne pointed out that in a few years the *Kind Words Series*, already owned and published by the Southern Baptist Convention, would bring a revenue of $15,000 annually. Continued publication of this *Series* would insure sound literature for Southern Baptist churches. Such literature would bring the rising generation into sympathy with the Convention. Publication of their own literature would inspire self-respect.

In his amazing historical summary, Hawthorne even recalled that the earlier Sunday School Board had run straight into the Landmark controversy. That controversy, to be sure, caused the gathered throng in Fort Worth to recall the influence of the great Landmarker himself, J. R. Graves. The thought of Graves immediately brought to mind his chief opponent, R. B. C. Howell.

The involvement of Graves in the publication history may have suggested at once the significance of his origin, for Graves was not a native of Tennessee or even of the mid-South. He had come to the Volunteer State by way of Kentucky from his native Vermont. This reminder of geographical origin was a subtle implication of the risk in relying on outside sources for literature.

In Nashville, Graves had become the apostle of Land-

markism. Thus, this controversial personality at once required of Southern Baptists that they consider in any publication enterprise the risk of theological and especially of
ecclesiological questions. Landmarkism had almost wrecked
the Convention on the rocky shoals of a narrow ecclesi-
astician and a rigid authoritarianism. Now in Fort Worth
in 1890—or at any time a religious body contemplates
establishing a publishing enterprise—consideration must be
given to the risk of running afoul of unwanted doctrine.
If Southern Baptists were to launch a publishing enterprise,
they would do well to remember the Landmark debacle
of the 1850s and the 1860s.

Of course, all of these historical matters were not in the
short and somewhat impromptu speech of J. B. Hawthorne
in Fort Worth. But, his historical allusions may have brought
many of these interrelated factors into the thoughts of the
messengers in Fort Worth.

Ultimately, the Landmark influence had brought about
the removal of the first Sunday School Board from Greenville
to Memphis in 1868, where at that time Graves himself
resided. The new secretary of the first Sunday School Board,
T. C. Teasdale, also a Northerner, was a Landmark disciple
who had been chairman of the Mississippi Baptist Convention Committee which attempted to call on R. B. C. Howell
in Nashville in an effort to bring about a reconciliation
between Howell and Graves.

Thus, there were many delicate, interesting, and important interrelated circumstances in the minds of the messengers at Fort Worth when they came to confront the issue
raised by J. M. Frost. Frost himself with naivete had projected this question into their consideration.

Really, it is remarkable that even at that one annual
session the Convention could arrive at a mutually accepted

compromise. When the committee came together, as required by Frost's own motion, the question at hand was far from simple. What the committee did, and the action the Convention ultimately took, was a tribute to their diligence, their perception, and their dedication to ministry through the teachings of God's word.

It is well just here to note some relationships of those who comprised the committee. Chairman, of course, was the man who had introduced the resolutions, J. M. Frost. Just previously to assuming the pastorate in Virginia, he had been the pastor of the Convention president, Jonathan Haralson of Selma, Alabama. Others on the committee included J. L. Lawless; C. Durham, corresponding secretary in North Carolina; Joseph Shackleford; E. C. Dargan, of South Carolina, who later became an editor with the newly established Sunday School Board; J. H. Kilpatrick, outspoken moderator of the Georgia state Baptist convention; W. E. Atkinson; F. H. Kerfoot, professor at Southern Seminary and later to succeed Isaac Taylor Tichenor as corresponding secretary of the Home Mission Board; M. A. Bailey; Joshua Levering, industrial tycoon of Baltimore; and B. H. Carroll, then pastor in Waco but later to be the head of the Bible Department at Baylor University and the founder of Southwestern Baptist Theological Seminary. The other two, who brought the minority report from the committee, were J. B. Gambrell, editor of the Mississippi *Baptist Record,* and W. S. Penick of Louisiana.

The details of committee interaction of these men representing thirteen states expired with the end of their eventful lives. *Not one of them revealed what was said in those sessions.* Frost's motion which brought about their appointment was made on Friday afternoon, the first day of the Convention. Their report came to the Convention the following Monday. Thus, they had all of Saturday, and any of Sunday that they might have spared from worship exercises. Their report was a special order at 10 o'clock on Monday morning.

What we know about their considerations is revealed only from the printed reports which they made. That really is sufficient. In the strange and strong interplay of personalities, of emotions, of judgment, it is really too much to expect that they could have ever come to any final decision, much less to a unanimous agreement. The report they made is really exactly what under the circumstances thoughtful persons surely must have expected.

Eleven of them, through their spokesman, J. M. Frost, presented what was called the First Paper. The other two, with Gambrell as their spokesman, offered a Second Paper.

These two said that they never could come to agreement within the committee. Therefore they begged "leave to submit the following minority report." They felt that the Convention had acted the previous year in sufficient measure for the time being. They saw no need before the contracts expired the following year to make an ultimate decision about the disposition of the existing publications, the *Kind Words Series*.

In view of this strenuous and persistent disagreement, the First Paper proposed what Frost and others called a compromise. It made no recommendation concerning the issue which had been proposed by Frost, that the Convention set up a board of publications. Rather, it simply suggested that a Sunday School committee be named to oversee the publication of the *Kind Words Series* and to study Sunday School work and needs. They recommended what was really to be an interim Sunday School Committee.

They also clearly, and first of all, recommended that the

Home Mission Board be relieved of the publication of Sunday School materials. The contracts both with the printers and with writers should be transferred from the Home Mission Board to the newly appointed committee. Meantime, while continuing the publication of the *Series,* the committee was charged with the responsibility of canvassing "the whole subject of catechetical instruction" and also the survey of Sunday School needs. The committee was also to suggest suitable books for use in the Sunday Schools, in addition to the *Series* itself.

When these two papers were presented and had been discussed, the Second Paper or the minority report was rejected by a vote of 176 to 419. Then, the First Paper, or majority report, was adopted.

Thus, the Convention had done no more than adopt an interim compromise. The editor of *The Religious Herald* was quick to point this out. But, with great pleasure, the same editor also quickly reminded his readers that the compromise was a fulfillment of the *Herald's* early position, that the Home Mission Board should be relieved of its publication responsibilities.

Meantime, what was the attitude of the Home Mission Board leader himself, Isaac Taylor Tichenor? Remember, he had been the man who, in Selma, Alabama, had planted the idea of "making our own literature" in the mind and heart of the young Selma pastor, J. M. Frost. Now, in the Home Board's annual report to the Convention in 1890, Tichenor had taken account of the possibility of setting up another Convention board with publication responsibility. Tichenor stated very clearly that the attitude of the Home Board was positive in this regard. If the Convention elected to establish another board which would relieve the Home Mission enterprise of publications responsibility, that, wrote

Tichenor in the Board's annual report, would be cordially accepted as valid Convention decision. On the other hand, if the Convention decided to retain the existing arrangement, the Board would gladly comply in responsible management of the publication interests. There is really no evidence at any point of any contention by Tichenor to hold on to the *Kind Words Series* as a Home Board activity, nor even any reluctance to surrender it if that should be the Convention decision. That was the spirit of the man who first planted the idea of "making our own literature." J. M. Frost ultimately did become indeed the father of the new Sunday School Board—but Tichenor was the grandfather! It just may have been the biggest thing Tichenor ever did.

When the messengers left Fort Worth in May, 1890, they still held the burning idea of what to do about publications. They had made strides in the direction that they would ultimately go. But they had not yet resolved the question. Still the matter was the topic of debate among Baptists everywhere. A year would pass before that issue of overpowering importance would be resolved. How it was accomplished in a dramatic session in Birmingham is reviewed in the next chapter.

8

Victory in Birmingham

If the account of Fort Worth sessions was indeed comprehended in the actions of two men in that session—James Marion Frost and James Bruton Gambrell—the full record of the conclusive action the next year in Birmingham in 1891 is even more intensively the record of those same two stalwarts, plus the dramatic influence of the current Southern Baptist patriarch, John Albert Broadus.

Indeed all of the events of 1891 in Birmingham can be properly and accurately reported from the viewpoint of the two principal actors, Frost and Gambrell. Even a contemporary report can be fully and properly related by the two principal characters themselves, one written some twenty years later and the other given at the time by the journalist himself, J. B. Gambrell.

The dramatic and even spectacular interpositon of Broadus on the scene is told pointedly, and yet meaningfully, also by Frost and Gambrell.

First, look at the scene in Birmingham, as reported at the time in the Mississippi *Baptist Record*, by its editor, J. B. Gambrell.

The Magic City in the red hills of Birmingham was crowded by Southern Baptists in May 1891. Gambrell, in his columns, stated that it "is a great convention." Visitors

according to the *Record* "are as numerous as the delegates."
Attendance the previous year in the Western city of Fort
Worth had reached a near record, with 781 messengers
present for those sessions, the number being surpassed only
one previous time, at the sessions in Richmond in 1888.

Now in Birmingham a record enrollment was on hand.
Gambrell reported that "855 delegates answered to their
names." Others would appear later. The Mississippi editor
predicted that more than one thousand would be on hand.
O'Brien's Opera House was "packed to the doors and standing room was at a premium in the galleries" before the
Convention was called to order. The editor was also impressed with the attendance of ladies from all parts of the
South.

In the chair was Judge Jonathan Haralson of Selma, Ala-
bama, "whose forte is in the dispatch of business." After
President Haralson called the Convention to order, "and
the uproar was stilled," the first business was the enrollment
of messengers which consumed more than an hour. The
Mississippi paper reported that the first order before the
Convention was the sermon, the second the report of the
Home Mission Board, and the third the report of the Sunday
School Committee. This committee had attracted the principal interest of the messengers. For the report of that
special committee, Editor Gambrell said that a great many
more were on hand than could "get in the Opera House."

"For three years past," he wrote, "the question foremost
in interest at the convention was what to do with the *Kind
Words Series.*" Gambrell pointed out that "the tentative
arrangement of a year ago could not give the denomination
peace, and therefore would not last. It had been decided
very decidedly that the *Series* would continue; but the lease
plan was continued and everything evil in the situation had

free play."

"The Sunday School Committee appointed a year ago," Gambrell wrote in the *Record*, "made their report as required, which report was referred to a committee of one from each state. The Senior [editor] was on that committee and Dr. Frost of Virginia was chairman. It was a strong committee of men with strong convictions. After many hours of prayer and conference we reached an agreement. The report was passed with practical unanimity by the Convention.

"Only Dr. Broadus spoke, and he for conciliation and peace. He followed the line on the report and said that it was perfectly clear that Southern Baptists are divided on this question. For twenty years he would have been glad if all of us could have agreed to get our literature from one existing source; but he had known all the time that we would not do it. It was impossible to agree, and, therefore, we must accept this situation and let everyone do as he pleases.

"It was a very happy putting of the case and made way for the adoption of the report without debate."

This is Gambrell's account at the time. Now skip over twenty years to see the same actions as given more dramatically by J. M. Frost in *The Sunday School Board, Its History and Work*, published in 1914. Frost recalls the scene at "the hour of the special report" on Monday morning when "the great hall was crowded to the limit." Frost himself, chairman of the special committee, says that he reached the hall with the report fresh from the committee. The committee had struggled for many hours from the time of its appointment on Friday evening to the very hour on Monday morning when the report was to be given.

Again, the special committee was composed of one from

each state. Frost, representing Virginia, was the chairman, and J. B. Gambrell, representing Mississippi and still the spokesman for the opposition; H. S. D. Mallory, Alabama; A. J. Holt, Arkansas; S. M. Province, Florida; F. C. McConnell, Georgia; W. S. Ryland, Kentucky; B. W. Bussy, Georgia; Joshua Levering, Maryland; R. W. Rothwell, Missouri; L. L. Polk, North Carolina; J. M. Mundy, South Carolina; W. C. Grace, Tennessee; B. H. Carroll, Texas.

This committee named Gambrell and Frost as a subcommittee to formulate the report.

What a strange subcommittee! The two men represented the exact opposite views. One was possessed by the deep conviction of the idea of a board of publication which he could not give up. The other, just as definitely, represented an opposing view.

In his book written more than twenty years later, Frost describes their experience: "It was a serious task. We represented opposing sides of the issue, but realizing the mighty moment into which the denomination had come, and what would be the far reach of our action in the settlement of the impending question, we set ourselves to the task with the best that was in us. We both cherish in sacred memory the experience of those days in working to that end. I make no effort to set on record a recount of what went on between us, though it is fresh in memory after all these years. After much conferring together, and at the close of a conference which lasted practically all day, he proposed to let me write the report and even name the location of the Board, provided he could write the closing paragraph. When the report was written, and he added his words, they were accepted, provided he would let me add one sentence."

Thus the two champions, representing opposite views, came to an amicable conclusion.

What they wrote, in what Frost referred to as "our upper room in the Florence Hotel," tells the story of this denominational development. Here is that paragraph as recorded in the *Southern Baptist Convention Annual, 1891:*

"In conclusion, your committee, in its long and earnest consideration of this whole matter in all of its environments, has been compelled to take account of the well known fact that there are widely divergent views held among us by brethren equally earnest, consecrated and devoted to the best interest of the Master's Kingdom. It is, therefore, recommended that the fullest freedom of choice be accorded to every one as to what literature he will use or support, and that no brother be disparaged in the slightest degree on account of what he may do in the exercise of his right as Christ's freeman. But we would earnestly urge all brethren to give this Board a fair consideration, and in no case to obstruct it in the great work assigned it by this Convention.

Signed by the Committee."

Frost, in his account, simply stated that the work he and Gambrell did in that hotel room "was the outcome of an effort by two men, believing in each other, and differing widely at the start, and in the end thinking themselves together." He adds, "That report stands in the minutes of the convention, just as it was finished that day" in their room in the Florence Hotel, "without any shadow of doubt but what an unseen presence was molding the two into one."

Frost also recalls in his book the dramatic scene in O'Brien's Opera House when the Convention adopted the report of this special committee. Indeed the committee chairman, Frost, was detained until the final moment in order to present the report he and Gambrell had written to their larger committee. Their committee had adopted it unanimously but the chairman was late in reaching the meeting place.

"At the hour of the special order on Monday morning," Frost writes, "the great hall was crowded to the limit. I reached the hall fresh from the committee, and was unable to enter the building, but was literally lifted in through a window and made my way to the platform as the report was already being called for."

Rumor had it that there would be a "battle of the giants." At least a hundred messengers, no doubt, were ready with speeches in hand, each intent upon having his say as soon as the committee chairman had concluded his report. Then a strange and dramatic thing happened. We have already given Gambrell's contemporary account of what happened. Here is the way Frost described it twenty years later:

"I had scarcely finished reading, with the audience hushed in stillness, and before I could address the president, Dr. John A. Broadus was on the platform and in command of the occasion. And in less time than I can write it, he had brought the Convention to a vote. No one knew how, but all saw it done and acquiesced in the decision.

"He did what few men may do once, but perhaps no man would try a second time. He did not move the 'previous question,' for that would have failed, but he accomplished the same result through the sheer power of his influence, and brought the Convention to vote without debate and I make no effort to reproduce what he said. He made no speech, besought that others would not speak—put a lid on the volcano, and waited to see what would happen—a sublime moment of heroism and faith. It was masterful in the noblest sense. Some thought his action part of a scheme, but not so. He no doubt had his purpose and plan well in mind, but if he ever told anyone, the secret has never become known to me."

That daring feat was accomplished by the power of his presence as the recognized patriarch of Southern Baptist life. For a generation John A. Broadus was the recognized spokesman on any and every issue before the Convention. He had been the corresponding secretary of the first Sunday School Board when he and his compatriot, Basil Manly, as professors in the struggling seminary at Greenville had initiated the publication effort of Southern Baptists. Now for a generation he had moved to the place of eminence among Southern Baptists as leader of their theological school. But, he was also the spokesman in any and every session when Baptists confronted a grave issue.

In Birmingham, at a delicate moment, he did what no other man could have done. He simply asked that the assembled and restive messengers restrain themselves from speaking and vote on an issue that had been the chief consideration now for a decade. There had already been ample time for consideration. Messengers knew their minds. Everyone wanted to speak. But it was the patriarch himself, John A. Broadus, who alone could influence them to vote without debate.

With only thirteen dissenting, the Convention adopted the report of the committee. It called for the establishment of the Sunday School Board. The committee also designated its location in Nashville, Tennessee. Thus writes Frost: "The end had come; the Sunday School Board had been established, with all that it meant for those years of struggle and for the succeeding years into which joy we have come."

Already the previous year in Fort Worth the Home Mission Board had been relieved of responsibility for publication of Sunday School literature. At the same time the determination of the Convention to continue the *Kind Words Series* had been definitely made.

Now by Convention action the Home Board was finally relieved of a significant responsibility, the ongoing project being assigned to another agency. In 1890, the Home Mission Board's report had reflected a positive attitude toward Convention decision, whatever it might be. In 1891, the Home Board's report made no reference to the possibility of Convention action to create a publishing board. There was only this commendation of the influence for missions of Sunday School literature:

"The Board cannot refrain from expressing its gratification at the result of the mission lessons contained in our Sunday-school series. We have the most undoubted testimony, coming to us unsought, that the information they give about the Convention, and the work of its Boards, is awakening an interest in mission work in our Sunday-schools not only beneficial for the present, but which promises much for the future."

In Birmingham in 1891, the Convention had acted conclusively. In adopting the report with the dramatic paragraph written by Gambrell, and the final sentence added by Frost, the Convention had acted within the framework of traditional Southern Baptist polity.

The final paragraph written by Gambrell stated the traditional polity of independence of action, and of church autonomy. The Convention would not, did not, attempt to abridge the independence and autonomy of the churches. Each church was free to secure its literature as it pleased. The Convention would not abridge that right. Every church

would be free to buy its literature when it pleased, within
the principle of independence and of local church autonomy. In its board of publication the Convention would not
coerce.

No church would be required to buy its literature from
the new Board, but at the same time the Convention, in
sincerity, was assigning a responsibility to its own agency.
Every opportunity would be given to the new Board to
produce literature to meet the needs and the wishes of the
churches. All that is within the traditional principles of
independence, of autonomy, and of responsibility were in
that significant last paragraph written by Gambrell and the
meaningful final sentence added by Frost. Churches were
free and would always be free to secure their Sunday School
literature from any source at the option of the churches,
but the Convention through its established publication
agency would with responsibility provide literature suited
to those needs and optional wishes. In one paragraph, and
one final sentence, these two men wrote Southern Baptist
policy and polity in the publication of literature.

A fair and concise evaluation of that action of the Convention was written by Gambrell himself in the Mississippi
Baptist Record for May 21, 1891: "It was clear that a majority of the Convention wanted the [*Kind Words*] *Series*. They
were entitled to have it. It was better to put it on a solid
basis than to continue it in such a way as would invite
agitation. It was better to have a Board.

"But it was necessary to have the Board composed of
brethren whose surroundings, past record and spirit would
justify the hope that a conservative policy would be pursued.
It was, also, wise to so place and make up this Board, that
it would be easy for all the brethren to fall in with it. This
condition was met by locating the Board in Nashville and

placing the management in the hands of brethren wholly unaffected by past troubles, and yet brethren also who will push the work.

"A distinct declaration of rights will be found in the report. The divided state of sentiment among us is recognized, and the right of everyone to take and support what literature he prefers, without being in any way deprecated is acknowledged and insisted upon. We wrote this ourselves and without it neither the committee nor Convention would have agreed.

"But a fair consideration of the claims of *Kind Words Series* is earnestly asked. We wrote that too. The Board was made up with great care and with special reference to the carrying out of the broad spirit of the Convention. No truer, nobler men can be found in all our bounds. The president and a majority of the Board have always favored *Kind Words*. There is a minority who have been on the other side; but they will labor earnestly to bring all of the good possible out of the situation. They are for the most part young and vigorous; the class of men who must shape the destiny of the great state of Tennessee as it enters upon its new era of development.

"We are perfectly satisfied with the new status, and pledge the Board our earnest support along the line of the report. Every personal element has been eliminated. This interest has been placed on a high plane of benevolence, and it is to be pushed not as against something else, but for the good it can do.

"It will have a vigorous management and we have no doubt of its financial success.

"Let everyone understand that this is not a blow at the American Baptist Publication Society. There is no suggestion of antagonism, but to the contrary.

"We have hope that the brethren will generally accept this settlement as final, and that on this generous policy we may inaugurate a new era in Sunday school work in the South."

In the next chapter we will seek to discover the significance of locating the new Board in Nashville, the meaning of that location in the psychology of that community background, its significance to the denomination as seen in the crosscurrents of history that made the community what it was.

9

Why Nashville?

In the now famous understanding between J. B. Gambrell and J. M. Frost in Birmingham in 1891, by which the significant final paragraph to their report was written, it was also agreed that Frost, by the suggestion of Gambrell, would name the location of the new Board.

In consequence, it is well-nigh certain that Frost himself named Nashville. Yet, in his book, *The Sunday School Board, Its History and Work*, he has very little to say about this choice. He does remark that "there were strong undercurrents, and for the most part favorable to Louisville." It, indeed, would have been a personal inclination of Frost to suggest a location within his native state of Kentucky. Georgetown, where Frost had spent many of his younger years, both in college and while his father was pastor in that college community, is only a short distance from Louisville. Moreover, the first Sunday School Board had been established in Greenville, South Carolina, largely through the influence of two professors in Southern Seminary, John A. Broadus and Basil Manly, Jr.

At the time of the establishment of the new Board, Broadus, now residing in Louisville, was writing what was expected to be a primary Sunday School publication, a catechism for older children. Thus, to have located the new

Board in Louisville, hard by the Southern Seminary, and in proximity to the already enlisted Broadus, would have been a logical choice. Frost offers no explanation as to the decision not to go to Louisville.

Almost certainly one reason was that Louisville was on the fringe geographically, and not at the center of Southern Baptist territory.

Indeed the location of Nashville, in the center, although less than two hundred miles farther south, was one of only two reasons suggested by Frost for the selection of the Tennessee city. He simply remarked that it "holds almost the exact geographical center of the Convention territory—from Maryland to Texas and New Mexico, a very important item in the conduct of our business."

He added that "Nashville itself is a delightful city and that experience ultimately proved that a wiser choice could not have been made." Writing twenty years later, Frost felt that through the years "the conviction is very strong, and perhaps with everyone" that the selection of Nashville was fortunate.

The second reason given by Frost for the selection of Nashville is characteristic also of the man's logical turn. Nashville, he states, "is by far the largest printing center in the South, and one of the largest in the whole country. This location of technical skills," says Frost, "has been of immense help in many ways, and promises to serve the Board yet many years to come."

Nashville had been prominent as a printing center for almost a hundred years. At the turn of the century, in 1800, the small community on the Cumberland River was already known for its numerous publications, particularly weekly newspapers and printing houses which served the book trade. In those early years printing in Nashville was encouraged and almost sustained by patronage of the state. Government required the issuance of legal documents to the degree that a principal activity was that of the state printer, operating in the state capital. The first printing press in the state had been brought on horseback from North Carolina. This early printer was attracted to move over the mountains to engage in printing for the state. His first operations were on the downward slopes of East Tennessee, but in due time printing for the state was done on presses in Nashville.

The single greatest boon for the printing industry in Nashville had been the coming in 1854 of the Methodist Publishing House. This was coincident with the general upheaval among religious bodies in the country which resulted in the establishment of separate Southern branches of the Christian denominations. When the Methodists experienced their separation, South from North, their big printing establishment was moved from Philadelphia to Nashville, both equipment and personnel. Thus, a thriving printing establishment of the Methodists had given a great boost to the printing industry in Nashville. The location on the Cumberland River in Tennessee of the Methodist Publishing House proved to be a great asset to Baptists in their new Sunday School Board. Almost certainly the location in Nashville of the Methodist Publishing House was a strong factor in the decision in 1891 to locate the Sunday School Board in those same environs.

These two practical considerations, says Frost, led to the location of the new Board in Nashville—the geographical advantage of being near the center of the Southern Baptist territory, and the presence in Nashville of superior technical personnel for the operation of the printing enterprise. These are the only two reasons stated by Frost in his report of the coming of the new Board to Nashville.

But, undoubtedly, there were many other factors, sociological, technical, psychological. As is true of any other community, there were many interrelated facets in the background of Nashville to give it distinctive personality. Moreover, no doubt these varied and interrelated circumstances influenced the decision to locate the publishing board of Southern Baptists in Tennessee's capital city.

It is certainly true that Frost's primary drive was to meet a great need of a growing denomination. In doing so he would be consciously influenced primarily by the two practical factors he named, rather than being moved in any recognized way by the subtleties of community personality.

But, still it is strange how the background of the community in Middle Tennessee had a logical, albeit subtle, relationship to a publishing enterprise.

One of those background factors was the early determination of R. B. C. Howell, when he first came to Nashville in 1835, to support his pastoral ministry through publications. When Howell visited Nashville the previous year and agreed to accept the pastorate, he did so with the understanding that he would launch a Baptist paper. This was by agreement with the leaders of the church. When Howell arrived in Nashville in January 1835, he at once launched *The Baptist*.

This was an uncanny recognition, even in those frontier times, of the need for publishing the word. It was also prophetic of a place to be served, of a mission to be performed by the Nashville community in the years ahead. Publishing, even as early as 1835, for Baptists in the South was recognized at least by one prominent leader, as being inherent in successful projection of the kingdom of God in the lives and hearts of men.

But even before that day, the Nashville community was astir with foregleams of the significance of publishing. Howell himself, in his unpublished *Memorial to the First Baptist Church of Nashville,* graphically describes salient aspects of the throbbing community. It was peopled in the main by newcomers, westward pressing populations moving across the mountains and into the beckoning West and Southwest. These who came into the section from abroad brought many ideas, notions that were provocative not only of discussion but even of tension. As these many people from many places moved into the community, their ideas were expressed in tumultous encounters.

Howell in his *Memorial* points out that the chief topic of exchange was on religion. The primary questions discussed on the frontier, in the marketplaces, and in the crossroad stores, were theological. In the main, the hardy frontiersmen took definite positions, either of Calvinism or of Arminianism. The sharp cleavages in religious views, says Howell, were on the subject of divine sovereignty. Was it absolute and purposeful, without possibility of human alteration? Or did the human will act responsibly and finally? Extreme Calvinism was indeed the firm conviction of many in that day, but also there were others just as determined to believe and to indoctrinate within the framework of a free human will.

In the great developing section of Middle Tennessee religion was the daily and fixed concern of the masses. Moreover, the people were obsessed to verbalize this intense preoccupation with definite religious views. They talked their beliefs. They published their doctrine. They stated, both orally and in writing, their views on matters of the spirit.

In those earlier years there was a decided anti-mission

spirit. This was extreme Calvinism. The vocal Calvinist in his commitment to total divine sovereignty of God, saw no need of the human element in spreading the Kingdom. God could do this in his own way, in his own will, without human agency. Thus anti-missions was a widespread position. Communities as well as churches and individuals became popularly known as anti-missions or missions.

Prominent spokesmen, even in the pulpits, were fervent in their opposition to missions. One such prominent preacher was asked if he had made a contribution when Luther Rice had made an appeal for the work in Burma. He replied that he did not have a counterfeit half dollar on his person to put in the offering and he certainly would not give to missions any real money.

Another significant force of a somewhat kindred nature was the so-called reform movement of Alexander Campbell and of his father, Thomas Campbell. Campbellism was very strong in Middle Tennessee. Indeed, Campbellism had exercised such an influence in Nashville that practically the entire congregation of the First Baptist Church had embraced its teachings and had taken the building and the records just a short time before Howell came to that pastorate. This was also done in other communities. Campbellism, too, was a rigid doctrine, at the beginning without purpose to establish a new sect or even to depart from the Baptist denomination, but rather simply to "reform" the doctrine and the government of Baptist churches.

Significant in the background of the Middle Tennessee community was the Landmarkism of the middle of the century. As pointed out in chapter 7, J. B. Hawthorne, in his historical summation in Fort Worth, had noted that the first Sunday School Board had to face the question of the Landmark movement. The leader of the movement was J. R. Graves, who succeeded Howell as editor of *The Baptist*, and soon instilled an authoritarianism which had devastating effect in Middle Tennessee and indeed throughout the South.

The Landmark effort was aimed primarily at refuting the pedobaptist position and establishing the "old Landmark" views. These rigid authoritarians would recognize no ministers as valid gospel preachers except those who had been ordained by true New Testament churches. New Testament churches, of course, were only those who subscribed to the Landmark views.

Landmark leadership illustrates again the complexity of crosscurrents from afar which contributed to the psychological, the sociological, and the religious factors of the Nashville community. Landmarkism was both cause and effect. J. R. Graves brought determined views to infiltrate a strongly vocal community. He and those who framed the Landmark movement represented a strong purpose to publish established doctrine.

Nashville, as the location for a publishing enterprise, offered a background of intense verbalization on religious subjects. The community developed in an atmosphere of provocative interaction on belief.

Nashville was chosen out of practical and simple considerations. But there are subtleties in the community development of earlier years related uncannily to the verbalization involved in publishing. The association between that background and the accepted responsibility of a new publishing board cannot escape the student of these developments. Nashville was named as the appropriate locale for a publishing enterprise. Even her background denoted vigorous engagement in knowing the doctrine and proclaiming it with great spirit.

In view of scant resources provided to get the movement going, would great spirit suffice? The next chapter details the amazing answer.

10

Brick Without Straw

"The Sunday School Board was set to its task May, 1891, without means—absolutely without means. True, it was to have the *Series* of periodicals, and these were of great worth, but they were not available for many months yet to come." This is the declaration of the man who came to the responsibility of establishing this publication venture, absolutely without capital investment to enable it to get started. J. M. Frost, who came on July 1, 1891, as the Board's first corresponding secretary, declares this astounding economic circumstance in his book, *The Sunday School Board, Its History and Work.*

The Kind Words Series, to which he refers, dated its origin to 1866, when the initial Sunday School paper, *Kind Words,* had been launched by the first Sunday School Board. In 1886, *Kind Words* had become a *Series* with the addition of other Sunday School publications. By this date Sunday School publications were the responsibility of the Home Mission Board after the first Sunday School Board had been suspended in 1873. When *Kind Words* became a series, their publication was by lease arrangement between the Home Mission Board and a private printer, the Board receiving a royalty through the lease contract of $1,000 a year.

At the 1890 Convention, *Kind Words* series was assigned

to the standing Sunday School Committee with headquarters in Louisville. The contract with the Atlanta printer was continued, including the $1,000 a year royalty. This royalty was the total income for expenses of the Sunday School committee which operated out of Louisville as publisher of the *Series* from their appointment at Fort Worth in May 1890, to the meeting in Birmingham in May of the next year.

With the establishment of the new Sunday School Board the lease contract was still in operation and would be to the end of the year. The lease contract with the Atlanta printer for the *Series* was still binding. The new Board could not publish literature for sale to the churches until that contract would expire at the end of 1891—six months after the Board began to function as a Convention agency on July 1, 1891.

Thus, the new Board was set up without any funds for current expenses—salaries, correspondence, travel, or even office space. Actually, with the coming of J. M. Frost as corresponding secretary on July 1, the agency was indeed a one-man Board—one lone man and he without an office. Space for a desk was by the generous courtesy of *The Baptist and Reflector*, E. E. Folk, editor. It was not a very impressive beginning situation—a one-man Board, and he occupying a desk in the borrowed corner of an editorial office.

Immediate expenses—the bare minimum—included the moving expenses of the new secretary from Richmond, Virginia, to Nashville, Tennessee, his salary of $250 a month effective as of July 1, his travel expenses to get the new Board established in the understanding and favor of the constituents, and office incidentals. One item very important to the new secretary was the proud letterhead—The Sunday School Board of the Southern Baptist Convention, Nashville, Tennessee. This, said Frost, identified the Board as an institution in the community. It added esteem for the man, for his office, and for the new Board.

The thought of initiating a denominational publication enterprise, with no funds made available to meet these basic first expenses is so astounding as to be almost unbelievable. This lack of any money from any source, or even the prospect of realizing funds from the new business for nearly six months is a circumstance difficult to comprehend.

That was not all of the well-nigh unbelievable economic stringency. The new Board also fully understood that the Convention would tolerate no accumulation of debt as a liability of the Convention. Thus, a new board, a publishing enterprise, with inevitable immediate financial need, was established without resources for these immediate necessities, plus the clear understanding that its favor with the authorizing Convention could be maintained only if it entailed no debt.

There is another way of stating these rigid requirements more positively, and with clearer actuality. The Convention had established a publishing agency on the principle of self-support. Its only source of revenue, even at the very outset, would be from the literature offered for sale to the churches. No funds were provided for the immediate operating expenses. From the very first day, the new Board must earn its own way. In earning its own way, the Board's managers and particularly the corresponding secretary were keenly sensitive to the necessity of maintaining its expenses within the revenue realized from the sale of literature. It must not come to the Convention the next year, 1892, with any debt!

Board records for 1891 provide some understanding of the nature and size of the immediate expenses. Upon the first meeting of the new Board following the Birmingham Convention the corresponding secretary's salary was set at $2,500 a year. This same amount was being paid to the corresponding secretary of the Home Mission Board and to the corresponding secretary of the Foreign Mission Board. Immediately, the new Sunday School Board set this salary, even before the election of a corresponding secretary. It was offered to the man first elected, Lansing Burrows, who declined the position. Then it was confirmed by the Board upon the election of James Marion Frost.

In addition, the Board also elected Frost to be the editor of *The Teacher* at an annual salary of $500. Thus, the corresponding secretary of the new Board was offered a total remuneration of $3,000 a year, which was $500 more than was being paid to the men in like positions of executive responsibility with the two mission boards.

Moreover, the new Sunday School Board engaged John A. Broadus to write a catechism for children. By a cooperative arrangement with the American Baptist Publication Society in Philadelphia, the writer was to receive a total of $500, half of which was to be paid by each of the two publication agencies. Samuel Boykin, who for many years had edited *Kind Words*, was elected editor of its other publications at a salary of $1,500 a year. These two salaries plus the honorarium to Broadus totaled a commitment of $4,750 by a Board which had no prospect of income from sales until December, 1891.

These commitments, rather sizable to an infant agency, must be seen in the light of economic potential. To the new Board was assigned the *Kind Words Series*. In the 1891 discussion in Birmingham, the Sunday School Committee had proposed to accept a renewed contract with a printer who had now offered to increase the annual royalty from

$1,000 to $5,000. Proponents of the Convention's own publishing agency pointed out that the *Kind Words Series* could be printed at a total cost of no more than $20,000 a year, with a projected income of at least $30,000 a year. A royalty of $5,000 a year was only half of the expected earnings that could come to the Convention's own publishing board.

This current expectation of at least $30,000 a year from the *Kind Words Series* had been bandied about repeatedly in Convention sessions. The popular expression was that the *Series* had a gross yearly value of at least $30,000. This potential, with the expiration of the existing printing contract, was now a potential economic resource to the new Sunday School Board.

Moreover, the economic potential was directly related to the size of the constituency and the number of schools in the churches needing literature. It was fairly well established, even by uncertain statistics, that there were some 1,500,000 Baptists in 17,000 churches cooperating with the Convention. These churches had around a half million Sunday School members, all of whom needed literature for their weekly class instruction.

No more than about half of the churches at that time reported Sunday Schools. The Sunday School Board thus had the potential of providing literature for some 8,500 Sunday schools in about 17,000 churches with a half-million "scholars" enrolled from a total membership of a million and a half. Altogether it was a sizable potential to attract the favorable expectation of adequate financial support. This potential indeed was primary to the Convention's overwhelming vote to establish their own publication agency.

It was expressed even by the chief spokesman for the opposition to the establishment of the Board, J. B. Gambrell. He wrote immediately in his editorial columns in the Mississippi *Baptist Record* that the financial success of the new Board was assured. Even the man who spoke most vigorously in opposition was sure that the new Board would have adequate income.

The potential was indeed adequate. But the question still remains as to how an agency thus constituted without any financial resources would be able to operate for nearly six months. Its first income would begin to arrive with orders for literature in December of 1891. How did the new Board make ends meet? Was the income beginning in December adequate to meet the commitments? Was the Board able to pay expenses in its first year? At the Convention in May 1892, did it face the embarrassment of reporting a debt?

Actually, the existing minutes of the Board meetings give no clear answers. There is no conclusive explanation as to how the Board met its financial commitments beginning in July and continuing to the next year. The annual report of the Board made to the Convention the following May does give a very positive conclusion.

The immediate expenses, July to December, would have been a minimum of about $2,000—salary of the corresponding secretary, $1,500; honorarium to John A. Broadus, $250; incidental office expenses and travel of the corresponding secretary, perhaps $250. Printing bills presumably would not be due until after January 1. The salary of the editor of the *Kind Words Series,* Samuel Boykin, was paid by the printer to the end of the lease contract. From what source did the new Board meet these minimum expenses?

The only clue given by J. M. Frost is this sentence in his little book: "Money which the Secretary chanced to have in hand, but which belonged to another, was used temporarily to meet immediate and pressing necessities."

This is the only explanation of the possible source of

money to meet the minimum immediate expenses. Evidently that money which Frost "chanced to have in hand, but which belonged to another" assuredly would have been personal funds.

But neither Frost in his book, nor Board minutes still extant, nor the annual report of the Board to the Convention, confirm or explain the source of these funds which were used to meet "pressing necessities."

Only from family sources has it been known that the money to operate the Board in those months came from a family inheritance of Mrs. J. M. Frost. This oral explanation has long been circulated among those who have been acquainted with the early operations of the new Board. But there is no written or printed confirmation to be found in existing historical sources. The oral report that J. M. Frost borrowed from his wife's inheritance has been published, but not with a firsthand confirmation from historical documents.

Even as recently as 1966, Mrs. Marian Keegan, archival assistant in the Sunday School Board's Dargan-Carver Library, attempted to verify this long-standing family understanding. According to a note prepared by Mrs. Keegan this is the record as confirmed by the family:

"Mrs. J. M. Frost let Dr. Frost have $5,000 as a loan to the Sunday School Board to help begin its work in 1891. She had inherited this money from her father.

"Dr. J. M. Frost made the above statement to Miss Ethel Allen, his secretary, several times during her term of service with him. Miss Allen was secretary to several of the executive secretaries of the Sunday School Board: J. M. Frost, I. M. Van Ness, T. L. Holcomb, and James L. Sullivan.

"Marcellus Frost, son of Dr. Frost, told Miss Allen that his mother let his father borrow the $5,000 from her to start the Sunday School Board.

"Marcellus said he once asked his mother after Dr. Frost's death, 'Did Father ever pay back the $5,000?' She replied, 'He said he did.'

"Howard E. Frost, another of Dr. Frost's sons, told Mrs. G. Kearnie (Marian) Keegan that Mrs. Frost let Dr. Frost have her $5,000 inheritance to start the Sunday School Board.

"Both of these, Marcellus and Howard, are still living here in Nashville (2/2/66).

"Just this morning I talked with Miss Ethel Allen to verify this information."

From these oral reports and the written note from Mrs. Keegan, it appears that J. M. Frost used family money for the six months, July to December 1891, to meet the "pressing necessities." Why is there no record of the transaction in the Board minutes? We can only surmise that the Board's corresponding secretary felt it unnecessary to put in a permanent record this family transaction. Evidently he used his wife's inheritance, repaid it as soon as funds were available, and made no record of the loan or of its repayment.

The annual report given to the Convention the following year, in May 1892, contains no record of this family transaction. It was a personal use of family inheritance by the Board's corresponding secretary, a private, personal loan from wife to husband and repaid without any entry in the Board's record.

There was another source of money to meet "pressing necessities." During the year, according to the annual report made the following May, the Board had borrowed on two occasions from a Nashville bank, a total of $1,050, all of which, too, had been repaid before the closing of the books for its first year of operations.

Writing over twenty years later, Frost proudly added that the money borrowed that first year was "the only sum the Board ever borrowed."

Money from the sale of its literature began to arrive in the Board offices in December, covering orders for the first quarter of 1892. It was a dramatic moment for the corresponding secretary, and his two employees, a mail clerk and a bookkeeper, when the first order was received in the still-borrowed office space!

In his own direct way, J. M. Frost pointed out that the Board as a business "would necessarily have an income-making power—a money value, but whether large or small will depend upon circumstances." He added that "diligence, painstaking care, every possible precaution and watchfulness" were exercised. Evidently, the money which "he chanced to have in hand" met the need for "pressing necessities" for nearly three months or until the latter part of September when "the Board secured from the First National Bank two short-term loans, the notes being endorsed by individual members of the Board." These loans "carried us through until receipts began to come in early in December from the January issue of the periodicals—$5,000 for the month of December—and the notes were paid when they came due. I recall well my excessive delight the first day our receipts amounted to $100."

The financial statement at the close of the year showed a total income of $20,800.66. Included was the sum of $302.24 left over by the Sunday School Committee. From the sale of periodicals, merchandise, advertising, and for missions the Board had received $19,272.50. The balance came from short-term loans obtained from the banks.

Cash payments included, for printing, paper, binding, mailing, and postage, $9,692.11. For manuscripts, including the exposition of lessons, the Board had paid $777.50. Salary of the secretary for ten months had totaled $2,083.33; payment to the secretary as editor of the Convention *Teacher,* $466.67; to the editor of other periodicals (Samuel Boykin) for five months, $600; to the bookkeeper and clerks for five months, $868.50. Salaries this first year had totaled $3,968.50. The statement shows the payment of the loan obtained from bank of $1,250. Cash payments had totaled $19,734.88, which when subtracted from the receipts of $20,800.66 left a balance on hand of $1,065.78.

Thus, in this first year of operation, the Sunday School Board had fully met all of its expenses and had come to the end of its first year with over $1,000 on hand. It had done so on the new self-sustaining principle, all of its expenses being met through the sale of literature.

It was indeed a remarkable record of financing under a unique self-sustaining plan, without contributions from any source for the work.

The secretary records that "it was a grave question whether the Board could cover its first year's expenses and reach the Convention in May free of debt. No one thought it could. Many were the anxious days and nights which came and went. Sometimes debt seemed certain, inevitable, as we worked, watched, waited. But when we had closed our books April 30, the end of the Board's first fiscal year we had paid all bills due and anticipated all bills coming due in the near future, and had on hand a balance of over $1,000. This was a surprise to us all, and threw a new light on the future."

Thus, he ends his own brief account of the beginning: "So the work began and so the work went on."

The creation of the Sunday School Board brought Southern Baptists face to face with the nature of the Convention's denominational structure. This, of course, had been confronted back in 1845, and once more in the era of recovery after the Civil War, but now it was even more sharply focused with the creation of the Convention's third Board. The remaining chapters will deal with Nashville as a thoroughfare, a means to an end.

11

Nashville Becomes a Highway

The design for a publication board is spelled out very clearly by J. M. Frost in *The Sunday School Board, Its History and Work,* to which frequent references have already been made. Even more pointedly, that design is stated in the Board's first annual report, which Frost presented to the Convention in 1892.

Writing in the strenuous days of establishment, Frost in neither instance said that he would discuss the appropriate functions of a denominational agency in the framework of Convention structure. He made no effort to contrast convention structure with society structure.

It would be expecting too much to assume that he would do so. The energy the initiator would overtly address to a new enterprise would not be one of definition. This was too philosophical in nature for an activist who was driven to establish an enterprise. His main concern would not be to define, but to energize, to establish, to develop. But in that very development he would succeed in direct measure to his basic understanding of appropriate function as related to an ongoing general body within which the new agency was to operate. While Frost did not feel compelled to define the difference between convention structure and society structure, yet in a very real sense his operations were based on that clear perception.

To give this implicit definition a figure of speech, we may here relate the title of this book to the subject of this chapter. The book deals with the significance of the establishment of the publishing enterprise. That subject is in the two figures of the title, ROAD TO NASHVILLE. Now, in this chapter, the goal is to realize that Nashville (the publication activity of Southern Baptists) is not an end in itself, but rather is a means to an end.

Never is a thoroughfare justified from internal considerations. A highway in essence is a passage, not the goal at which the traveler aims to arrive. The Board, as instigated by Frost at the very beginning, was designed to be a means to a goal, to an end. The justification for its existence would never be found within the agency itself, but rather in the ultimate aim which the Board would serve. In the mind of the chief instigator, Nashville from the outset, was a highway, a thoroughfare, a means to an end.

In realizing this perception of its purpose the Board must be made to fit into the genius of convention structure. In that structure all measures, activities, and enterprises work together to realize one key or central aim. No one of the Convention's agencies should become an end in itself, but all together in cordial commitment were designed to serve the same end.

J. M. Frost, very clearly and definitely, spelled this out in his brief account of the establishment of the Board, which he wrote some twenty years after the fact, and also in his first annual report to the Convention prepared at the close of the fiscal year in April 1892. That annual report, the first given by the infant Sunday School Board, made clear the cordial relationship of the new agency to the ongoing total and inclusive purposes of the Convention. It does not point out the difference in a convention structure and a society structure, but it shows clearly the way in which the new Board was set to function to serve all that Baptists were bent on doing in their Convention organization.

The Sunday School Board had a great and distinctive field of service, but it was to engage in that service always in conjunction with the Convention's other agencies and in coridal cooperation with them toward the same common goal. This Frost made crystal clear in that first annual report.

First and foremost, this cordial cooperation in a common enterprise would be achieved through publication of Sunday School periodicals. Thus, in that first annual report, Frost named the periodicals already being offered by the new Board. There was *The Teacher,* a monthly magazine, which in the upcoming months would offer a series of articles on missions (written incidentally by F. M. Ellis of Baltimore, who had opposed the establishment of the Sunday School Board); another series on Bible characters; still a third on the structure of the Sunday School in the churches; and a fourth by B. H. Carroll on "My Infidelity and What Became of It."

There were also quarterlies, graded to the interest and spiritual competence of Primaries, Intermediates, and the advanced. Still offered as a popular reading magazine was the long-established, and well-known, *Kind Words.* The new Board offered, even at the beginning, *Lesson Leaflets, Child's Gem, Lesson Cards,* and *Bible Lesson Pictures.*

Very proudly, the corresponding secretary asserted that these periodicals, "though much in advance from what they were, will be improved from time to time, both in literary merit and mechanical excellence." As Bible instruments of the Convention he added that in fostering their use the Convention did but support its own enterprise.

"Here is a property," wrote the secretary, "this Series of Sunday-school Periodicals which belongs to the Convention, and which the Convention, through its immense constituencies, can make an engine of tremendous working force."

Even in awarding the printing contracts, Frost asserted that the Board was serving the total interest of the Convention. Thus, the contract for printing the periodicals had been given very carefully on the basis of exact bids, the printers sustaining "no relation whatever to the publications save only as printers, and their contract covers all expenses from the setting of the type to the mailing of the Periodicals including postage. It is a printing contract in the strictest sense, and eliminates all private gain and all private interest. Any profit accruing belongs not to an individual Baptist or to Baptists simply in a general way, but to the Southern Baptist Convention in particular and as embodying the organic and organific life of the denomination." "This," wrote the secretary, "is emphatically your enterprise and . . . if success comes to it as it is now coming, every other enterprise in the whole field of your operation will feel its quickening impulse. Every order which comes to the Board at Nashville for Sunday school supplies is a direct contribution to the treasury and the missionary work of the Southern Baptist Convention. Our hearts are stirred as we think of what you may do with this great agency for good. Brethren, throw yourselves upon the confidence of your constituency, and invite them to join you in the work of the Sunday-school Board, and give you their support in this as in the Home and Foreign Boards."

In presenting a statistical statement, Frost admitted that "our best efforts only show how difficult it is to get correct and complete statistics." He said that "the following table is made up with great care" although there were "conflict-ing authorities." In fifteen states, the District of Columbia, and Indian Territory there were 681 associations, 17,416 churches, with 1,394,951 members, but only 8,862 schools with 455,137 "scholars."

"This is the best table that can be had," wrote the corre-sponding secretary, "not only as to its correctness but as giving the best possible showing of the condition of the Sunday-school cause among our churches. When one thinks of what has been done he rejoices; but thinking on what needs yet to be done his soul is moved within him; for after this best showing nearly one-half of our churches is without Sunday-schools, and in some states the condition is painfully otherwise. This means destitution that is appalling. The study of the figures merely is enough to make the heart sick; but what is to be said when we recall what these figures really mean! . . . Surely an organized effort should be made to bring about an improvement of this condition in churches where no schools exist, and also in the schools already existing. To lift up to a higher plain [plane] the whole Sunday-school condition within our bounds, as to general religious development and training in [Christian] work, is a matter of the very greatest moment, not only to the Convention but to the cause of Christ generally. This responsibility rests upon the Convention and can never be shifted nor met save by yourselves. To this great work the Sunday-school Board is especially committed, and earnestly asks for your most liberal support. So important is this undertaking that if the Sunday-school Board can accomplish it, the Convention could afford, out of its own treasury, to pay all the expense for an indefinite term of years. It would be like the farmer who empties his granary on the fertile fields, scattering that he may gather. The Board has its heart on this work; and the work is on our hearts. But no other support is asked save only sympathy and prayer and co-operation and patronage. This is what we desire of the Convention, and hope the Convention may request it of the churches and Sunday-schools."

At the very beginning Frost sensed the money-making potential of the publication business. Even before *Kind Words* became a *Series* that same little paper had "supported itself in all its expenses, and at the same time paid off an indebtedness against the Convention of $6,000, and then brought into the treasury an annual income of $1,000 royalty."

This had been the financial record of the one single paper, *Kind Words*, until 1886. Then, on being combined and enlarged with other publications, Frost pointed out that the *Series* had doubled in its gross income, from $16,000 the first to $32,000 in the last year.

"But what about the new venture?" Frost asked in his official report to the Convention. "Will it bear the strain of the new and larger expense?" Frost pointed out that "the Board began its life and work . . . with nothing in its treasury and with no immediate resources." Indeed the Board had been "practically without income from May until December, at which time we began to receive orders for 1892. Our expense account in part is for eleven months while we have receipts for only five months, December to April."

In those five months the gross income had been over $19,000, from which revenue the Board "has met all of its obligations" and "we have no indebtedness." For this record, Frost showed justifiable pride.

"It was expected," he admitted, "and indeed we ourselves expected to come to the Convention with a deficit, but instead, after having met all our expenses, . . . we have over and above all expenses a balance to our credit."

With this early success to give assurance for the future, the secretary said that "in the coming year we wish to improve our literature which will of course increase the expenses." Still he predicted that the additional expenses would be met with relative ease and the literature would still "yield a handsome fund for missionary purposes."

That assurance, as he pointed out, rested on increased circulation. "As the circulation of periodicals increases," the confident secretary stated, "it increases the missionary fund; and as the pastors and churches and Sunday-schools give the Board their support, they will increase the circulation, and so increase our missionary power, and that too without loss or cost to themselves, or without hindering other departments of Christian work or benevolence."

Directing attention to the new Board's support of missionary work, Frost pointed specifically to how it would support the Home Mission Board. Even missionary enterprises, he said, should be firmly established on sound business principles. Thus the new Board proposed to establish its work to bring in revenue that would aid the missionary work throughout the South and in cooperation with the existing state organizations. "We wish," he wrote, "to do something to relieve the vast destitution. . . . This is a work deserving the expenditure of money; it will yield immense returns and will at the same time be an untold blessing to hundreds and thousands in the years to come."

Frost thought particularly of how the Board would contribute through giving literature to new work. "Great good can be accomplished," he prophesied even then, "by furnishing literature to mission schools . . . in such a way as will be most stimulating to awaken a missionary spirit and

we have responded to every application which has come
to us and promptly filled the order in the literature that
was asked."

He admitted that this was "only a small beginning, but
it is surely a beginning, and will be greatly enlarged as
our resources are increased." Through this contribution of
literature he said that the new Board "will become a powerful ally to the Home Mission Board."

The perceptive Sunday school leader saw also the relation
of the new agency to "the Convention's Foreign Mission
interests." Granting that the new Board's field was primarily
among the children, he pointed out that through the Convention literature "we will endeavor to develop in them
the missionary idea and missionary spirit. This," he insisted,
"is of immense importance; for in the Sunday-schools of
to-day are the missionaries of the future for the home and
foreign fields, also the future pastors who will determine
the character of the churches in the future, and even future
members who are to support all our work at home and
abroad. The Sunday-school therefore must be in touch with
the Convention in all its missionary enterprises; and the
Convention must lay its foundations among the children
. . . . To put your hand upon the Sunday-school is surely
to put your hand upon the future movements and energies
for bringing in the kingdom of the Lord Jesus."

In a mellow, but determined, mood he added: "We have
consecrated your literature to this great end, and are aiming
to make it intensely missionary, as to missions in general,
and especially as to the missions of the southern Baptist
Convention. We desire to make the Sunday-schools and the
homes and the hearts of the children, great centers of missionary power."

One specific means of doing this was the strategic use

of a regular section in *Kind Words*. This young people's paper, Frost wrote, "beautifully illustrated and ably edited, gives the fourth page to missions in each issue, both of the weekly and semi-monthly editions. This page is under the editorial management of Miss Alice Armstrong (a sister of Annie Armstrong), of Baltimore, who has shown herself gifted and efficient, and is in the interest of the Young People's Department of the Woman's Missionary Union. It makes *Kind Words* pre-eminently the Convention's missionary paper for the Sunday-school and the home, with missionary information told in a way attractive to the young . . . . This is an immense power for the furthurance of the gospel at home and abroad. There could scarcely be a more powerful way of reaching the children and impressing their tender heart and plastic mind with the great missionary thought and need and duty . . . . Here is a leverage for power if the denomination will throw upon it the weight of their hand and heart."

Warming even more in his sustained enthusiasm, the young secretary added with evident fervency: "It is manifest that the Sunday-school Board through the power of its periodicals, may become a great factor in our denominational machinery second indeed to no other force in its influence upon our denominational life. it becomes a missionary power on home fields and foreign fields through its missionary literature. Who can foretell the results simply in increased contributions to the boards of the Convention, when you shall have two, and three, and four generations of men and women who almost from their cradle have been trained to think missionary thoughts, pray missionary prayers, and make missionary sacrifices in contributions laid at the Master's feet?"

Turning slightly in another direction, he added: "But

there is another way which in its far-sweeping influence surpasses all money considerations, and is simply immeasurable in its power to tell upon succeeding generations, namely the cultivating and growing in thousands of children, not only the missionary idea and spirit, but the missionary himself, who shall tell the wondrous story of redeeming love among the nations of the earth. Brethren, this great enterprise which you have entrusted to the Sunday-school Board is not a scramble and squabble for literature, but something in every way high and noble, and with your endorsement and support in Convention assembled and in your churches and Sunday-schools the Board may do a work of which the ages will be proud."

That expected support in "Convention assembled" Frost received from three committees which had been requested in the Sunday School Board's annual report. These committees were appointed in the 1892 annual sessions, and each commended even with enthusiasm the beginning shown by the Convention's new Board.

The Committee on the Business of the Sunday School Board was "impressed that the Board has been very careful in the making of its contracts, and has also energetically pushed the business." The five months covered in the report had "yielded a good profit," giving the committee reason to "turn most hopefully to the future."

The Committee on Periodicals of the Board, too, was pleased with the quality of the editorial work and especially of "the missionary set and trend" which would give value that "cannot be overestimated or unduly emphasized."

The report of the Committee on Spheres of Work of the Sunday School Board was read by the chairman, Robert J. Willingham, who later became the longtime corresponding secretary of the Foreign Mission Board. He read in part: "Experience has proven that the Sunday-school is a wonderful developer of Christian activity, not only good for children, but grown people as well. . . .

"The development and extension of this work means, to a great extent, the future development and extension of our churches. Within our bounds one million, three hundred thousand Baptists, with hosts of little ones and attendants, are to be trained in God's word and work. The literature to be used is, of course, very important, and we feel well pleased with the success of the Board in this direction. But let it be distinctly understood that the work of the Board is not simply in supplying Sunday-school literature to pay a revenue. It is to awaken, develop, organize and strengthen our churches in the great work of teaching God's truth to young and old . . . . We consider that one of the best features of our 'Convention Series' is that it is putting our missionaries and mission work upon the minds and the hearts of our young people. They are thus linked to the great work of missions—the work of all others on earth to-day. . . .

"Vast fields lie out before us to be cultivated. Our Board has a great work to do. The faithful training of the young means much, very much for the advancement of God's kingdom. Let the Board have our fullest sympathy and most earnest co-operation."

The final paragraph of Frost's first report of 1892 is a remarkable and convincing summary of the Board's purposes. It gave assurance then of the positive and assuring direction down the beckoning highway which the new Board proposed to travel. The new secretary was sure of divine blessing and gracious direction in the work that had been started.

"If the leadings of Providence can ever be read and interpreted," Frost asserted with calm confidence, "God's hand is surely in this movement, his favor has surely been upon the work. He has turned the hearts of the people as no other power could have turned them; and instead of the Board's being destructive and a stirrer-up of strife, it now promises to be a unifying element in our denominational life and enterprises." Certainly there was supreme relief and exquisite delight in the facts which had made it possible for Frost to say this, less than twelve months after the victory in Birmingham.

Continuing, he asserted, "All opposition and strife and discord are gone—or seem going. It is marvellous in our eyes and has filled our hearts with exceeding joy."

This impressed the new secretary of the new Board to anticipate even greater blessings to come: "God is opening a great door to the future for the Baptists of the South, and laying upon them immense responsibilities. He has thrown difficulties aside and bids the great Baptist host to a forward movement—trained in one school, and having one Lord, one faith, one baptism, one great heart and purpose for bringing in the kingdom of the Lord Jesus, and sharing in the joy and glory of his coronation. The Convention, with its several departments, is yet a unit in organization and organic life, having responsibilities which are enough to fill an angel's care, and opportunities which are enough to make an angel's heart beat faster. We stand in the present, but we speak for the future; we work in the present, but shall gather and garner our harvest in the centuries and the ges and the eternities."

Thus, without saying so, J. M. Frost really had come full circle in the realization of the nature of the organization which Baptists were still in the process of perfecting. Back in 1845, a primary consideration was the nature of the body being then named the Southern Baptist Convention. What was its structure? How was it different from traditional Baptist bodies? Particularly, how was it distinct from the society structure?

Immediately following the Civil War, the question of survival for Southern Baptists again centered on the nature of the Convention. The struggle to define structure inhered in the inevitable conflict between the Home Mission Society of the North and the Domestic Mission Board (renamed Home Mission Board) of the Southern Baptist Convention.

Now, as Southern Baptists reached the final decade of the century, the structural question finally came more nearly to the point of resolvement. They were coming more surely to clarity of understanding between a Convention and a society in denominational structure.

Frost was pointing to that distinctive when he asserted that the Convention "is yet a unit in organization and organic life." It was becoming a denomination. It was becoming a denominational body embracing the total interests of God's people. Together they would function through more than one Board. Now, indeed, the Convention would function not only through the mission boards, but also through a publication board. The new publication board, like the mission boards, was no end in itself. It was a means to the same end to which the mission boards were committed. Indeed, the entire denomination through all of its agencies was committed to that same end. Through this kind of structure, and only through such a structure, could a great people together engage as one toward a common goal.

Putting the new Board, which he headed, very firmly in that connectional structure, Frost also wrote in that first report: "Of course the literature is essential, but only as a means to an end—a powerful means to a noble end."

Thus by polity, deliberately written into their structure

as a Convention, Southern Baptists together are committed to one great unifying enterprise. Nashville is a highway, simply a passage, a means by which God's people together work in one common mission to bring the kingdom of the world to become the kingdom of our Christ.

The continuing contribution of Nashville toward that mission will now be noted in the final chapter.

12

The Continuing Road

At this point, the present discussion could be appropriately concluded with a resumé of the development of the Sunday School Board in its unfolding years. Such a summation would detail the record of the vast circulation of the many first and later publications; an appraisal of the effect of this literature in teaching a people; an inspiring assertion of the support given by the Board through these publications to the Convention's missionary enterprises at home and abroad; to the even more significant far-reaching total support of the denomination; and finally how all of these impressive statistics contributed in these eighty-five years to the growing of a denomination.

Such an account has already been done, responsibly, effectively, and with cordial appreciation. It has been accomplished in at least three specific instances.

First, J. M. Frost himself looked objectively at the record. This he recorded by request after twenty years of the Board's operations, in a small volume to which recurring references have been made on these pages—*The Sunday School Board, Its History and Work*.

Second, at the conclusion of the Board's first half-century, P. E. Burroughs wrote with his characteristic admiration and zeal, *Fifty Fruitful Years*. This was a worthy tribute in 1941, when the Board celebrated the conclusion of a half century of service.

Third, *The Story of the Sunday School Board* by Robert A. Baker, published in 1966, is replete with detailed activities bringing magnificent accomplishment, along with inspiring summaries of those strategic achievements.

A similar historical condensation is unnecessary to this present treatment for an important reason. The historical account is inconsistent with the purpose of this volume. It does not contribute to the basic intent in these pages.

The title of this volume—note it carefully—is ROAD TO NASHVILLE. The emphasis is on that two-letter preposition, *to*. This account is simply a report on the road *to*—not the road *after*. The primary focus, therefore, does not involve the results of traveling that way in any summary look at the record.

There is still another significant aspect of what may at first appear to be an omission. It is unnecessary at any point since 1891 to sum up the record of these eighty-five years. It is unnecessary because, with uncanny foresight, that record was written at the very beginning. It is contained even in those resolutions written in the nighttime by J. M. Frost back in January 1890. He was given then, at the moment, an almost unbelievable realization. With remarkable foresight he spelled out in advance on that winter night the history of the publication agency proposed in his newly stated resolutions.

Since that time, the unfolding record has been but the step-by-step fulfillment through the agency being called into existence by the Richmond pastor on that January night in 1890.

The history of the Baptist Sunday School Board can be read in those 1890 resolutions. It was spelled out as to polity and policy. It was written into the initial proposal. In a strange sense Frost himself later craved the privilege "of saying in the simplest way, God touched me and I thought it."

All who have succeeded Frost have followed carefully, even minutely, in his train. The record that has followed has simply carried out the details, faithfully, diligently, even exhaustively. The specific programs of action were clearly in those resolutions.

Unnecessary now in view of good accounting offered appropriately at three strategic moments in history, but declared just as definitely at the outset in 1890, is the faithful record of the Sunday School Board. Simply needful in this conclusion is a recall of the strategic inclusions in that remarkable 1890 document. Alongside his proposed resolutions were comments written by Frost at the time and published in the *Religious Herald* of February 27, 1890.

First, implicit in the proposal to establish a board of publication would be the verbalization of doctrine by a denomination.

How often does some lay person express the need to understand doctrine, with some such remark as, "We do not know what we believe! What is our belief?" Such a comment is manifestly foolish. Of course, a person knows what he believes. A body of people knows its doctrine.

But they need to express it. This is implicit in the purpose of a publication board. Its very first duty is to state the doctrine of the constituents. This is the accepted responsibility of a publishing board.

Note that its purpose is not to formulate doctrine and hand it down to the people as a body of mandated beliefs. Rather, the purpose is to combine jointly by the people called Baptists their community of beliefs. Their system of doctrine would be published in literature offered as their own developed and developing doctrine. The body of instructions in the study of God's Word would be both jointly held and jointly expressed.

This was truly the first function of the proposed board, to state the doctrine of the people called Baptists. They, themselves, would produce it, organize it, publish it, and it would become the body of truth as held by Baptists and offered to their own people through their Sunday School literature. It would be written, edited, and published in their own joint publication enterprise.

Second, this publication of doctrine would be self-sustaining. While the first duty—that is, to elicit and combine their doctrine and publish it in Sunday School literature—was implied in the proposals, the practical policy that it should be self-sustaining was stated very clearly. The first function was implicit, but the second important practical arrangement was explicit.

There were six resolutions written by Frost on that January night. The six provided for "a liberal allowance for the conduct of its business." This would include salaries of employees, printing expenses, the provision of office space.

At that time, it was stated in the columns of the *Religious Herald* that the American Baptist Publication Society then had capital investments which totaled $750,000. When action ultimately was taken on Frost's proposal, not one dollar was provided as capital investment for these basic expenses.

Frost wrote at the very beginning that such expenses should be met by "a liberal allowance for the conduct of its business." This meant that the new Board had to anticipate very carefully what these expenses would be, and set the prices of its literature to bring in sufficient money to meet these ongoing expenses.

One instance of "a liberal allowance" was the salary the new Board voted for the corresponding secretary. That salary was set by a Board without any funds. With nothing more than the prospect of selling literature to churches, they made the salary of their chief executive officer $2,500 a year. This was the same amount then being paid to the corresponding secretaries of the Foreign Mission Board and of the Home Mission Board. In addition, the new Board elected the corresponding secretary as editor of *The Teacher* with an additional compensation of $500 a year. Out of anticipated literature sales they offered total compensation to their elected secretary of $3,000 a year, which was $500 more than being paid to each of the executive officers of the other two Convention boards.

The new secretary had no part in setting this compensation, for it was made by the Board of Managers on their own responsibility before J. M. Frost was elected to the position. It was a direct interpretation by the Board of Managers of "a liberal allowance for the conduct of its business." The same principle would apply to the other practical arrangements—printing contracts, provision of office space, employment of additional persons.

In all of its actions, the Board of Managers would carefully calculate anticipated expenses and make provision for meeting them by the prices charged for the literature to be offered to the churches. Those prices should be sufficient to meet these expenses in the "conduct of its business." Whatever might develop as to personnel salaries, printing contracts, work space would be included in the prices to be charged for the literature.

The resolution written by Frost in January 1890, provided

that these expenses should be met, not extravagantly but liberally. Frost himself, according to his own declaration, had no notion that he would be personally involved in the enterprise. Almost certainly he even then realized that there was a direct relation between the practical provisions for employees and the quality of their work. The same would apply even in the technical know-how of printers to be engaged. With uncanny insight the resolution called for "a liberal allowance."

The new Board, as written into the initial resolutions, was to be self-sustaining. Its total operations were to be maintained by the sale of literature. If this was not unique in religious operations at the time, it certainly was new for Southern Baptists. At that moment, they had no experience in maintaining a Convention Board in this way. The total activities of the proposed Board were to be sustained even from the very first day, not by any contributed money, but altogether from the sale to the churches of the literature which the new Board was to produce.

Third, the new Board was to support the Convention financially from this income. All of its income after this "liberal allowance for the conduct of its business" the Board should then allocate to the work of the convention, appropriating "as the Convention may direct from time to time."

It thus was anticipated at the very beginning that the publication enterprise would earn money for the Convention. It was even very specifically designated at the outset that all income thus earned should be "appropriated" into the work of the Convention. It was expected that the prices charged for literature would create a surplus that the Board would use in missionary endeavors. The prices would be set to bring in such revenue, revenue sufficient to meet all expenses "liberally" and beyond those expenses to build up income to be used in Convention work.

This was indeed a unique financial policy, to meet all expenses from sales, and in addition to provide financial support of other Convention enterprises.

Moreover, as Frost pointed out, support of the Convention would come through the promotion of Sunday Schools. In his article, Frost showed that the Sunday School movment received almost no support in the sessions of the Convention. This, Frost wrote, was a tragic neglect. He himself had made a careful study of the Convention annuals, which revealed that almost nothing had been done in recent annual sessions to "foster this great interest." Such neglect, he insisted, should no longer continue. The opportunities and possibilities through the Sunday Schools "are simply immense." At the last Convention of 1889, "this department of Christian endeavor is most conspicuous by its absence— even in the statistical tables."

Frost insisted that "it is of sufficient importance to deserve, and has grown to sufficient magnitude to require, a separate magagement—a Board of Managers charged with supplying proper literature, and by wise methods increasing the number and power of the Sunday schools, and bringing them in contact with the Convention by annual reports. No one can tell the immense outcome from such a management pushing this interest with agencies and forces such as are now at work for the Foreign Board and the Home Board."

Even at that early date of 1890, Frost was enthusiastic to believe that "there are several lines along which a Publication Board can operate for the greater development of even the best Sunday schools, and others in proportion." Frost was proposing the promotion of Sunday School work along with the publication of periodical literature as helps for the development of the Sunday School movement in all of the churches. This, he said then, would be the significant promotional work of his proposed new publication board.

Thus, he was proposing a new board designed, even at the beginning, to build a denomination. It would support the Convention financially. More significantly, it would promote the Sunday Schools as agencies of teaching and of denominational support.

This denominational support he felt at the beginning was strategic in the growing of a denomination.

The significance of the establishment of a publication board was written into its basic purpose of support of the Convention. At the very outset, the man who saw this need wrote it into his original resolutions. By remarkable foresight, Frost, in effect, wrote the history of the Sunday School Board in his initial proposal for its establishment.

Frost himself later wrote that "God touched me and I thought it." The experience became "an impelling power." He was "driven on with a conviction that could not yield."

It is no wonder that he dared not remain silent. It was to him a clear revelation. He could not fail to act on those divine orders. He was under mandate. He acted under compulsion from above. This was the origin of the publication agency. It was history recorded from the beginning. It was and is the divine origin of a publication venture which from the beginning was ordained of God. This was the clear impulse felt by Frost at the beginning.

Through the combination of these most significant factors, the Sunday School Board became the strategic instrument in Convention service. Uniquely, it was set to pull the constituency together. Thereby, the Board could be the agency to bring about the cohesion of God's people.

Through this inherent structural principle, the Board was the agency which greatly contributed to Southern Baptists' becoming a denomination. This was and is the distinctive service to Southern Baptists of the ministry of publication. It brings to fulfillment the solidity inherent in Convention structure rather than in society. It marks a distinctiveness possible with the establishment of a publication board.

Here is the great contribution of the Board which Frost led the Convention to establish. Thereby Southern Baptists could become indeed a denomination. When this thought possessed Frost, it really is no wonder that he could not let it go. It is now an occasion of deepest gratitude that he was thus compelled. God spoke to him and he could not be silent.

Selected Resources

Basic information on these developments are in the contemporaneous Baptist newspapers of the period, 1880-1900:

Biblical Recorder
Mississippi Baptist Record
The Alabama Baptist
The Christian Index
The Western Recorder
Religious Herald

Other Primary Sources:
Correspondence of J. M. Frost in the first years of his administration
Kind Words
Minutes of the Sunday School Board, 1891-1900
Southern Baptist Convention Annuals

Other Sources:
BAKER, ROBERT ANDREW. *Relations Between Northern and Southern Baptists.* Fort Worth: Published privately, 1948.

BAKER, ROBERT ANDREW. *The Story of the Sunday School Board.* Nashville: Convention Press, 1966.

BARNES, W. W. *The Southern Baptist Convention, 1845-1953.* Nashville: Broadman Press, 1954.

BROWNLOW, WILLIAM GANAWAY. *The Great Iron Wheel Examined.* Published for the author. Nashville, 1856.

BURROUGHS, P. E. *Fifty Fruitful Years.* Nashville: Sunday School Board, 1941.

BURROUGHS, P. E. *The Story of the Sunday School Board.* Nashville: Sunday School Board, 1931.

CATHCART, WILLIAM, editor. *Baptist Encyclopedia.* Philadelphia: Louis H. Everts, 1881.

COX, NORMAN W., editor, *Encyclopedia of Southern Baptists.* Nashville: Broadman Press, 1958.

DURHAM, JACQUELINE. *Miss Strong Arm.* Nashville: Broadman Press, 1966.

EVANS, ELIZABETH MARSHALL. *Annie Armstrong.* Birmingham: Woman's Missionary Union, 1963.

FROST, J. M. *The Sunday School Board, Its History and Work.* Nashville: Sunday School Board, 1914.

GRAVES, J. R. *The Great Iron Wheel.* Nashville: Graves and Marks, 1855.

JACKSON, WALTER M. *The First Hundred Years*—A history of the Selma Baptist Church of Christ. 1942.

MOREHOUSE, HENRY L. editor. *Baptist Missions in North America.* Philadelphia: Baptist Home Mission Society, 1883.

ROBERTSON, A. T. *Life and Work of John A. Broadus.* Nashville: Sunday School Board, 1900.

ROUTH, E. C. *The Life Story of Dr. J. B. Gambrell.* Oklahoma City: Published by author, 1929.